The Affluent Handbook

The Affluent Handbook

Understanding America's Top Income Quintile

By Matt Oechsli

Wealth Management Press
9800 Metcalf Ave.
Overland Park, KS 66212

First edition.

Designed and typeset by Sans Serif Inc., Saline, MI
Cover design by KCL Creative, Ramseur, NC
Printed in the United States of America

ISBN: 0-9656765-9-5

Contents

Introduction

Once upon a time, the name Cadillac was synonymous with luxury. Today's affluent baby-boomers, however, have forsaken Cadillac for BMW, Lexus, Mercedes, Infinity, Acura, etc., because they demand prestigious cars packed with performance, quality, value and service.

Cadillac's fall from grace stemmed from a failure to understand the affluent, which is rather strange, because there's nothing complex about understanding the affluent. They want to be served, and then served some more. They want top quality, their money's worth, and then a bit more. They shop at discount stores, but finding the cheapest 50-inch flat-screen plasma television is not their top priority: they want good value at a fair price.

Because most of today's aging boomers come from middle-class backgrounds, they tend to define themselves as middle class, regardless of their current lifestyles. A middle-class self-image is indelibly stamped into their subconscious. As a consequence, most do not view themselves as affluent. After all, there have been—and always will be—families with more.

As consumers, the affluent can be extremely demanding. They do their homework, actively use the Internet, and conduct thorough pre-purchase research. Because they've become the target of virtually every marketing campaign under the sun, the affluent have developed a "buyer-beware" mentality—i.e., they are a highly skeptical species. It should come as no surprise, therefore, that they don't like salespeople.

That said, the affluent offer an acre of diamonds for any company, service professional or tradesperson who invests time and resources in truly understanding their needs, wants, fears and expectations. You must address their needs and wants vis-à-vis the products and services you offer, and help them to overcome their fears—all while exceeding their expectations. Because aging, affluent boomers are a walking, talking paradox, they are not an assignment for the weak, the weary or the company looking for short-cuts. It is important to understand how they make decisions, their key motivators, what they like and dislike, and the games they tend to play, both with themselves and others. (By the way, the boomers don't like to labeled *aging* or *senior*—or any other adjective that suggests "elderly.") Those who remain ignorant of what makes the affluent tick will find themselves increasingly challenged to compete for their attention and their business.

Everything in this handbook is backed by comprehensive research, which The Oechsli Institute has been conducting for nearly a decade. We know how the affluent make major purchase decisions, and we've uncovered the key motivators that shape those decisions, and much more.

The bottom line is that if you work (or spend much time) with the affluent, you will be best served by acquiring a thorough understanding of their psychological profile. In demographics and social research, this is known as "psychographics"—analyzing specific market segments based on values, attitudes, interests and lifestyles.

Because aging baby-boomers are the wealthiest generation in history, with so much money in (or about to be in) transition, understanding their psychographic profile is a must. From our most recent research project, we were able to divide the baby boomer profile into *Four Key Affluent Motivators for Life's Decision Making:*

- Personal Health
- Family Health
- Financial Health
- Spiritual Health

After reading this book, you will find it difficult to listen to a politician, read a newspaper, watch the evening news, or look at an advertisement without thinking of these key affluent motivators. You will see the good, the bad and the ugly.

In today's world, the precise definition of the term "affluent" has been blurred. Is it Tiger Woods, lounging on his yacht so aptly named *Privacy*? Is it Bill Gates, funding his foundation with another couple hundred million dollars? Or is it the family next door with a three-car garage and a condo at the beach, which you rarely see because both parents are working? For most readers, the affluent are the people next door or the face staring back at them in the mirror.

This is what led us to conduct our research of America's top quintile income earners (as defined by the U.S. Census Bureau). These top 20% are the powerbase of Western capitalism. They pay the bulk of the taxes, spend the most money, and are intensely coveted by everyone who is marketing or selling anything.

My objective is to help you gain a better understanding of today's affluent. Make no mistake about it: because affluent boomers control vast sums of money, they need to be *very* well understood.

— Matt Oechsli

SECTION I

The Sphere of Affluence

1

Look into the Mirror

The top quintile of U.S. income earners accounts for 39% of all consumer spending.

—The New York Times, December 16, 2006

Remember the last time you had the privilege of visiting your local Department of Motor Vehicles? I do, and it was quite humbling. There's no priority given to drivers who own more vehicles, spend more money on insurance or pay higher taxes. And there's no express line to quickly renew your driver's license, which was my case. No, everyone is treated equally—like a number.

As the line crept forward, I grew more irritated with the situation and my own frustration. Everyone else seemed to be coping with the glacial pace. Why was I setting records for high blood pressure?

Then it struck me: I *expected* better. I expected high-level, personalized service—even from a government agency. As a hard-working, demanding, easily stressed and easily annoyed member of America's top income quintile, I felt *entitled* to better treatment. Unfortunately, this revelation didn't speed the line, but it *did* remind me of how important it is to understand the mindset of the affluent.

Like it or not, the affluent rule. Life is not fair . . . or maybe it's too fair. We are living in a meritocracy. Work hard and you will be rewarded. This is the creed of top quintile American wage earners. Understand them, and you will achieve a better understanding of yourself (or what you aspire to become). Fail to fully comprehend the complexities, the dichotomies and the insecurities of this powerful market segment and you will struggle—as an individual and as a businessperson.

Believe it or not, like it or not, ready or not, the affluent in America *are* different. The differences—in income, lifestyle, financial priorities, spiritual outlook and consumption patterns (to name a few)—must *first* be acknowledged and *then* understood to successfully market, sell or at least cope with a population segment that accounts for 50.4% of all national income.[1] It's also important to acknowledge and understand the "affluent facts" of life if you hope to gain a greater understanding yourself, because chances are that *you*—if you're reading this book—are a member of the top quintile. Using income, assets, demographics and psychographics as standards, you've probably already "made it," or you stand on the threshold of this ever-more inclusive club.

9 Million Strong and Growing

For the past decade, the Oechsli Institute has immersed itself in the top quintile, the world of the affluent. We've conducted many research projects in an effort to better understand them. Most recently, we commissioned an independent study ("Understanding the Affluent: America's Top Quintile Income Earners") to identify affluent consumers' key motivators. Based on this research, as well as that of other private- and public-sector sources, we've learned a great deal about what makes the affluent "tick."

In terms of income and tax burden, the top quintile:

- Earn an average pre-tax family income of $132,000.
- Controls an average of $250,000 in assets, excluding the value of their primary residences.
- As a group, pays 79% of all taxes.

[1] Carmen DeNavas-Walt, Bernadette D. Protor, Cheryl Hill Lee, "Income, Poverty, and Health Insurance Coverage in the United States." U.S. Census Bureau: 2005.

Table #1-1		
Average U.S. Income Levels and Tax Burders[2]		
	Average Income	**Tax Burden as % of Total Individual Income Tax**
Lowest 20%	$8,400	–2%
Second 20%	$21,200	1%
Middle 20%	$35,400	7%
Fourth 20%	$53,000	16%
Highest 20%	$132,000	79%

Naturally, these figures don't mean much when presented in a vacuum. So, consider the statistics in Table #1-1 to compare the financial and tax situations of the top quintile to those of the other quintiles.

Then consider that the top 1% of income earners in America has an average pre-tax family income of $719,000 and a group tax burden of 29%, while the top 5% of U.S. income earners enjoys an average pre-tax family income of $276,000 and pays 50% of all taxes. Little wonder, then, that our latest survey discovered that the #3 Financial Priority of top quintile income earners is minimizing taxes!

The good news: the number of affluent households in America has nearly doubled since the late 1990s—to about 9.3 million—and now represents about eight percent of all U.S. households. The larger affluent market, which includes households with a net worth of at least $500,000, has grown more than 50% (to 14.7 million) during the same time.[3]

These figures are a good starting point toward understanding the affluent, but they say little about demographic or psychographic differences, factors that reveal how the affluent (and aspiring affluent) differ from other Americans in terms of age, geographic region, attitudes,

---

2 From www.allegromedia.com/sugi/taxes, and summarized at www.cbo.gov/showdoc.cfm?index=1545&from=4&sequence=0.

3 2007 Phoenix Wealth Survey, p. 2 (from the TNS Affluent Market Research Program conducted by TNS Financial Services).

spending habits, economic, political and spiritual beliefs—factors that will make or break the professional hoping to successfully market to this segment. It's fairly easy (if time-consuming) to determine how much the wealthiest Americans earn, how much they invest, how much they spend, and on what. The *bigger* questions are: Who are these people? What are their values? What are their aspirations? What do they want from life, and how can you give it to them?

The Rich *Are* Different

The face of affluence is changing rapidly—literally and figuratively. Many of them are baby boomers who have just entered (or are about to enter) their peak earning years. This generation is currently the wealthiest in history, but Generation X is fast on its heels (though they are far smaller in terms of population).

Boomers spurred the entry of women into the professions, which has promoted more affluent, dual-income households. Throughout much of the 20th century, college campuses were dominated by men, and single-income-earning households were the norm. Today, women outnumber men on the college quads by about five percent, and more than 80% of the affluent are dual-income families.[4] The latest wave of affluent Americans is less likely to have inherited its wealth, and more likely to head single households than its predecessors.

During the past two decades, the doors to the "affluent clubhouse" have also been thrown open to growing numbers of African Americans, Asians, Latinos and other minorities. Although the high-net-worth market was still predominantly Caucasian in 2007 (78%), that's a drastic decline from 1990, when 90% of the affluent were white. And, thanks to the combined strength of boomers and Gen-Xers, the median age of high-net-worth households dropped from the upper 50s to 54 between 2000 and 2007.[5]

---

[4] Michman, Ronald D. and Mazze, Edward M. *The Affluent Consumer*, Westport, CT: Praeger, 2006, p 2.
[5] 2007 Phoenix Wealth Survey, p. 2

In terms of psychographics, this generation's experiences, values, concerns and buying preferences are often quite different from those of generations past. Many of today's aging boomers worry less about "keeping up with the Jones's" than about proving how *different* they are from the Jones's. Chances are, the affluent consumer cares more about the *quality* of a product than its perceived status, they enjoy the experience of the purchasing process nearly as much as the final outcome, and—even more important—they consider their time so valuable that they treat it as a luxury, something for which they are willing to pay big bucks.

Amid all this, birds-of-a feather do flock together. The affluent live in clusters. Geographically, they are more likely to live in the Northeast, Mid-Atlantic States or on the West Coast. If not, then they tend to live near major metropolitan areas such as Chicago, Houston, Memphis or Mobile.

> The largest metropolitan areas include the largest concentrations of people earning $100,000 to $199,000 a year. The affluent market buys jewelry, antiques, homes, vacations, and services such as financial planning, insurance, personal training and child care. For example, the number of certified financial planners grew from 23,350 in 1991 to 45,000 in 2003, according to the Certified Financial Planners Board.[6]

As I've already noted, and will continue to remind you, the vast majority of today's affluent are working Americans who happen to earn a healthy income, and very few are cloistered in gated communities, unwilling to associate with the "little people." Instead, many have emerged from middle-class backgrounds to become generators and earners of wealth. In all likelihood, the top-quintile Americans you know are self-made men or women.

Our 2004 APD Research[7] determined that 22.4 % of the affluent

---

[6] Michman, Ronald D. and Mazze, Edward M. *The Affluent Consumer*, p. 9.

[7] APD Research refers to *How the Affluent Make Purchasing Decisions*, a study commissioned by the Oechsli Institute in June 2004.

are business owners, 25.9% are self-employed professionals, and 44.9% are high-paid executives and commissioned employees (salespeople). Eighty-two percent of the affluent were between ages 35 and 64, with 11% under 35. Hard-working and entrepreneurial, these affluent consumers are goal-focused, committed to their careers, and willing to pay the price for achievement.

That "price" often takes the form of stress.

More than 75% of affluent business owners and self-employed professionals work more than 60 hours a week. They never have enough time to finish their work, so when making a purchase decision, they expect minimal hassles and maximum attention. In our APD Survey, seven qualities associated with making major purchase decisions were analyzed in terms of importance. Here's what we found:

- Two criteria stood above the rest: 83.3% said that offering the right set of features was very important; 75.8% said that being able to find the best possible option through careful evaluation and comparison was very important.
- 65.5% said that the opinions of immediate family members and trusted friends had a very significant impact on deciding where to look for options when making a major purchase decision, but only 37.8% said those opinions had a very significant impact on the *final* purchase decision.
- Once the search process is underway, the affluent place more confidence in their own ability to find information, sort through options, and make the final decision. Respondents also indicated that the Internet and trusted periodicals serve as major research vehicles.
- When given an opportunity to write in other criteria important to making major purchase decisions, warranties and guarantees won by a wide margin.
- Even though respondents were extremely price/value conscious, finding a discounted or sale price was not as critical to their final decision.
- Problem resolution and post-purchase service rated as having the

greatest impact on repeat business. Offering the lowest price ranked last.

- Respondents gave far less importance to reviews and testimonials than they did to the responsiveness of sales and service people.

Middle-Class Mindset

Many of the wealthy have little in common with their millionaire forbears of the 19th and 20th centuries—and for good reason. Most do *not* trace their affluence to the "robber barons" of the Gilded Age, but to the prosperous middle class that emerged after World War II. In other words, their incomes, assets and lifestyles belie more humble roots—roots firmly planted in middle-class soil.

About 93% of affluent Americans are self-made. They are CEOs, upper management, large and small business owners, self-employed professionals, partners in professional practices (doctors, CPAs, etc.), and successful high-commissioned salespeople. Although they tend to be hard chargers and consider themselves successful, as a rule they don't consider themselves "rich." Because of their drive and work ethic, however, they not only earn more money than most people, they have three times the amount of stress. Therefore, they don't like their precious time wasted, and they don't suffer fools.

> Demographically, the top-income households share many characteristics, one of the more notable being their origin in the decidedly middle class. . . . Today's affluent are living the American dream, with 90 percent coming from [the] middle-class. . . .[8]

Whether you're a financial advisor, attorney or luxury retailer—you must understand that, when dealing with today's affluent American, you're usually dealing with someone who clings to a middle-class mindset. The typical affluent believes in working hard, saving and

[8] Danziger, Pamela N. *Let Them Eat Cake: Marketing Luxury to the Masses—as Well as the Classes*, Chicago: Dearborn Trade Publishing, 2005, p. 40.

investing, maintaining his current lifestyle, planning for retirement, and is not convinced that he's a member of America's elite.

Perhaps this is because, as historian Paul Fussell asserted in his satirical sociological study *Class*, few people are capable of escaping the class status (and mindset) into which they are born. Although our children will adopt the mindset of the class in which we've reared them, says Fussell, our values, tastes, spending habits and worldviews have been stamped during childhood. It will be interesting to see if these affluent boomers ever *fully* accept their new status as members of the affluent or emerging affluent class.

This is a vital factor to consider when approaching the affluent in a business setting. It's not that they're grievously offended by designations such as "high net worth" or "wealthy": they simply don't buy it. There are a variety of reasons—real and perceived—to explain why they don't believe they're wealthy, and that's the subject of the next chapter.

Research Facts

- The top quintile earns an average pre-tax family income of $132,000, and pays 79% of U.S. income taxes.
- The top 20% of American income earners account for more than 50% of all consumer spending in the U.S.
- The majority of the top quintile does not inherit their wealth; 93% are "self made."
- The wealthiest Americans are largely concentrated on the East and West Coasts.

2

A State of Denial

Most of America's top quintile do not consider themselves wealthy.

—2007 "Understanding the Affluent" research study

Are America's top quintile members in a state of denial? How can families with multi-million-dollar homes and assets approaching (or exceeding) seven figures consider themselves anything but wealthy? Yet, aside from the "super rich" (households with assets of more than $50 million), the majority of affluent Americans don't consider themselves rich. Taken at face value, this self-perception seems absurd. But once you peel away the raw statistics and examine the mindsets, lifestyles and family backgrounds of the contemporary affluent, it makes perfect sense.

Chart 2-1

Financial Priorities of the Affluent
2007 Oechsli Institute Research

1. Meet current living expenses and obligations.
2. Maintain current lifestyle in retirement.
3. Minimize taxes.
4. Protect against serious financial loss.
5. Organize and coordinate all financial documents.

The above attitudes hardly seem like those of someone driving a Mercedes S-Class, who skis at Aspen and owns a second home in the Hamptons. They appear more like the priorities of middle-class wage earners fearful of slipping behind. Precisely! Many of today's affluent behave like middle-class wage earners, because (again) *that* is the background whence they came—a mindset from which they can't escape, no matter how different their circumstances are from their parents'.

In her book, DELUXE: *How Luxury Lost Its Luster* (Penguin Press, 2007), author Dana Thomas appears to have an issue with all of this boomer affluence as it relates to luxury items. She writes how the luxury industry "sacrificed its integrity, undermined its products, tarnished its history and hoodwinked its consumers." Thomas insinuates that the luxury brands she follows are now deceiving middle-class consumers into believing they are affluent. I would not be so fast to pass judgment.

The luxury industry is simply lowering the point of entry by also catering to this hard-working group of mature, affluent boomers who have middle-class roots imprinted in their DNA. It's foolish for the luxury industry to produce goods and services for "trust fund babies" when affluent boomers are willing and profitable customers, provided the bar is lowered slightly. Thomas appears shocked to overhear a well-dressed affluent woman voicing her interest in a fake designer watch. She'd probably also be shocked if she spent an hour shopping at Costco.

Incidentally, my wife (Sandy) recently expressed interest in purchasing a couple of fake designer watches. Maybe it's viral. Except that Sandy had a very logical reason, at least from her perspective: "This way, I won't have to worry about breaking my good watch or having it stolen." I must confess that I was a bit perplexed, but then amused, after reading Thomas's thoughts on the same subject.

Always keep in mind that most of your affluent clients and customers do not consider themselves wealthy. They don't like being referred to as affluent or high net worth. Why? Because they've been "worker bees" all their lives, and most continue to work *very* long and *very* stressful hours.

Terms such as "high net worth" or "affluent" are not anathema to top-quintile earners—in their minds, the words simply refer to someone else. Because most affluent boomers have forged their lifestyles using their own blood, sweat and tears, they were not "born on third base, thinking they hit a triple." They understand that there are plenty of other people who are wealthier. And those wealthier people constitute the "real" affluent, whereas they are merely middle class or upper-middle class.

> Mr. Steger, a self-described geek, has banked more than $2 million. The $1.3 million house he and his wife own on a bluff overlooking the Pacific Ocean is paid off. The couple's net worth of roughly $3.5 million places them in the top 2 percent of families in the United States.
>
> Yet each day Mr. Steger continues to toil in what a colleague calls "the Silicon Valley salt mines," working as a marketing executive for a technology start-up company, still striving for his big strike. Most mornings, he can be found at his desk by 7. He typically works 12 hours a day and logs an extra 10 hours over the weekend.
>
> "I know people looking in from the outside will ask why someone like me keeps working so hard," Mr. Steger says. "But a few million doesn't go as far as it used to. Maybe in the '70s, a few million bucks meant 'Lifestyles of the Rich and Famous,' or Richie Rich living in a big house with a butler, but not anymore."
>
> . . . When chief executives are routinely paid tens of millions of dollars per year and a hedge fund manager can collect $1 billion annually, those with a few million dollars often see their accumulated wealth as puny, a reflection of their modest status in the new Gilded Age, when hundreds of thousands of people have accumulated much vaster fortunes.[9]

[9] Gary Rivlin, "In Silicon Valley, Millionaire Who Don't Feel Rich." *The New York Times*, August 5, 2007 (www.nytimes.com).

According to some "working class" Silicon Valley millionaires, it's easy to get caught-up in a trap of always chasing people with more wealth. Said one person: "Here, the top 1 percent chases the top one-tenth of 1 percent, and the top one-tenth of 1 percent chases the top one-one-hundredth of 1 percent. You try not to caught up in it, but it's hard not to." There are continual pressures to spend more.

According to *Money* magazine, people do not believe they are affluent until they have $2.5 million in wealth. There is a denial of affluence even when the minimum income for this group is $75,000, with average total assets above $665,000.[10] Other evidence suggests that even a nest egg this large isn't enough to assuage the fears of some affluent earners, especially those who grew up poor.

For example, I know of a retiree whose assets place her *well* within affluent boundaries. She recently told her daughter, "There's no amount of money that could make me feel financially secure." This woman grew up poor in rural Pennsylvania. On several occasions during the 1940s and 1950s, her family depended on the father's hunting and fishing prowess to put meat on the table. Those memories stuck.

A Leveraged Lifestyle

There are plenty of tangible reasons why affluent Americans perceive themselves as less than wealthy. Many baby boomers have reached a fork in the road—one path leading to affluence; the other to financial challenges. Although most affluent boomers are self-made and work 50–60 hours per week, many live beyond their means, and could not survive two or three months without a paycheck. This is especially true of those living in America's most expensive locales—the Los Angeles, San Francisco and New York City areas—where even modest homes can sell for a million dollars. And don't forget: most of America's affluent are concentrated near big cities, where the cost of living is substantially higher than in rural areas.

[10] Marion Asnese, Andy Bornstein, and Douglas King, "The Changing Face of Affluence," *Money Magazine*, Fall 2002, pp. 42–56.

There is always the fear that a leveraged lifestyle might lead to financial ruin should there be an economic downturn or a personal reversal of fortune.

> Today's . . . debt bubble will . . . derail many baby boomer's retirement plans, and it's already hurting the generation that follows. Make no mistake: the statistics are ugly. As a nation, our borrowing is growing as fast as our wealth, we are loading up our kids with college debt, and we are continuing our spendthrift ways into retirement. Take the [recent] real estate boom. This windfall could have salved the financial wounds left by the 2000–2002 stock market crash. But instead, many homeowners . . . turned around and immediately spent their real-estate gains. Federal Reserve data show that the value of household real estate climbed 71% since [2001]. But mortgage debt grew even faster, up 75%, as folks cashed out part of their home's value when they refinanced or took out second mortgages.
>
> . . . Average debt levels are really increasing for children of more-affluent families, says Sandy Baum, a senior policy analyst at the College Board and an economics professor at Skidmore College. "Children of affluent families are now almost as likely to borrow as children of less-affluent families."[11]

In many ways, the "Father Knows Best" and "Leave it to Beaver" families of yesteryear—the ones who scrimped and saved to provide a better life for their children—have morphed into today's high-net-worth, dual-income families living in 4,000-square-foot homes with three-car garages, numerous bathrooms, swimming pools and formidable mortgages. The affluent of the 21st century may not feel rich for good reason, given the escalating costs of health care, tuition, transportation, etc. Ironically, this sometimes means that their less-affluent neighbors enjoy larger disposable incomes and may *feel* more financially secure.

---

[11] Jonathan Clements, "The Debt Bubble May Derail Many Baby Boomers' Retirement plans." *The Wall Street Journal*, March 23, 2006 (www.wsj.com).

> Thomas Stanley, chairman of the Affluent Market Institute in Atlanta and author of the book *The Millionaire Next Door: The Surprising Secrets of America's Wealthy*, says a typical wealthy person is likely to be a small-business owner who has lived his entire adult life in one city and who married once and stayed married. He probably spends no more than $400 for a new suit and does not own an expensive watch, while the higher income, lower net-worth individual drives an expensive luxury car.[12]

For example, a childless professional couple renting a one-bedroom apartment in Brooklyn, New York, with an annual household income of $75,000, incurs fewer expenses than a couple earning $250,000 in nearby Westchester County, where they're raising three college-aged children, paying a hefty mortgage on their $600,000 home and making installment payments on three automobiles. This leaves the non-affluent Brooklynites with more money to spend on luxury products and services.

I know a couple who used to live in Park Slope, Brooklyn. "Back in the day," they devoted much of their discretionary income to high-end vacations, including luxury cruises to Mexico, the Caribbean and Bermuda. In 2003, however, they purchased a home in Maryland, and have since dropped off the upscale radar, thanks to the expense of purchasing and maintaining a house and two cars.

Although these friends liked to splurge on cruises, this was essentially their only indulgence. As statistics demonstrate, it is the *genuinely* affluent who represent the lion's share of consumer spending—no matter how leveraged they may be. Your non-affluent neighbors may be upscale buyers, and this may blur the difference between the affluent and near-affluent, but make no mistake: the genuinely affluent DO spend more money overall.

A percentage of upscale consumers may earn as much as the affluent, but they don't have the assets to qualify. They are often concerned

[12] Michman, Ronald D. and M 2007 Phoenix Wealth Survey azze, Edward M., *The Affluent Consumer*, Westport, CT: Praeger, 2006, p. 17.

about upward mobility, keeping up with the Jones's, and may indulge themselves in a handful of luxury goods and services. They also have motivations, achievements and aspirations similar to the affluent. However, the upscale consumer has not yet "made it."

No Choice But Self-Reliance

Given their debt burden, it's no surprise that nearly everyone but the super-rich considers himself middle class. The "average affluent" still has to worry about money, albeit not as much as members of the lower quintiles. According to the 2007 Phoenix Wealth Survey, this "bearish" attitude is more widespread among younger generations of affluent Americans, those who fear that Social Security, Medicare and other government entitlement programs will wither by the time they retire.

> Gen-Xers have attained more wealth and at a younger age than the baby boomers and members of the "Silent Generation," but they are also the most uncertain about their financial futures.
>
> - Most of them will retire without a traditional pension plan;
> - They worry about Social Security and Medicare being around, and they are particularly concerned about spiraling health care costs;
> - They expect to be supporting one or more aging parents;
> - They will likely be living longer than baby boomers and the Silent Generation;
> - They know their assets could be affected by one or more perhaps severe economic downturns before they retire.
>
> In short, they view the responsibility for their financial future as being squarely, and heavily, on their shoulders.[13]

Many baby boomers as well as Gen-Xers have a profound fear of falling from the ranks of affluent, service-oriented professionals, due

[13] 2007 Phoenix Wealth Survey, p. 3.

(in part) to widely publicized (if not nearly as widespread) displacements that have accompanied globalization. Words like "outsourcing" and "downsizing" strike terror into affluent hearts the way "layoff" and "plant closing" once did (and still do) among the working class. The affluent recognize that the middle class in which they were raised is fast disappearing. Time was when a high-school education could land you a well-paid unionized job at an auto factory or steel mill. Now, a four-year undergraduate degree is the equivalent of a high-school degree, and probably worth less in terms of economic clout.

Value Still Trumps Fear

Despite their anxieties, the affluent are happy to pay top dollar to maintain lifestyles that—by all historical measures—can only be defined as luxurious. This fact has hardly escaped the notice of most service professionals and retailers, which is why the current market is essentially a bi-polar landscape: high-end retailers for the affluent and upscale; big-box discounters for the rest of the population; Ritz-Carlton for wealthy vacationers and business executives; Motel 6 for their less-affluent counterparts.

(This is not to say that you'll never run across your plumber buying a watch at Cartier, or bump into your financial adviser at Target—only that there's little left of the middle market.)

Of course, "luxury" is in the eye of the purchaser, and it's beyond the scope of this book to track—in detail—the ever-changing tastes and consumption patterns of a large market segment that doesn't walk in lockstep. Members of the top quintile are as different from one another as they are from members of the other four quintiles. That's why the remainder of this book is dedicated to identifying broad *categories* of attitude and behavior among the affluent—their fundamental likes and dislikes, and the do's and don'ts of selling to them.

Perhaps the biggest attitudinal difference defining top-income earners from everyone else is this: When it comes to making major purchase decisions, even in regard to hiring a personal tutor, attorney, financial advisor, accountant or personal shopper, value trumps price!

The affluent demand prompt, courteous and efficient (read: time-saving) services that provide experiences that are at best pleasant, at worst, offer minimal inconvenience. As a service provider or salesperson, this means *demonstrating* that you really care—not just saying so. The following is a dramatic, but by no means unique, example.[14]

Imagine investing $4 million with a financial advisor. Five years later, your nest egg has grown to nearly $ 6 million dollars! Your financial advisor has helped you earn a conservative 8% a year. That's what happened to Judy, and you might expect that she was pleased with her financial advisor. Not so. For the past three years she felt as though she was simply an afterthought, with her annual performance review the last two years conducted over the telephone.

It wasn't always like this. The first couple of years her financial advisor was in regular contact, and "even took me to lunch a couple of times." But somehow she got the impression that she was being taken for granted. She began calculating the annual fee her financial advisor was earning relative to the service, or lack thereof, she was receiving, and dissatisfaction became the theme every time she thought about her portfolio and her financial advisor.

Then she was introduced to Jack, a financial planner, by a colleague over lunch. Although Judy's portfolio was performing exactly as her financial advisor prescribed, she was dissatisfied. Why? Because within the world of the affluent, albeit performance being an important criteria, it is a "hygiene factor"—they expect a product (or portfolio) to perform as promised. But they also expect high-level service. And even though they come from middle class backgrounds and are exceptionally hard workers, when they purchase a product or a service, they want to be *wowed*—during the pre-purchase, purchase and post-purchase phases.

In Judy's case, her financial advisor was getting paid a fee of 1% a year. That's over $50,000 a year! No wonder why she was feeling neglected. Another interesting fact about the affluent is the old cliché,

[14] Ibid.

"Price is only a consideration in the absence of value." The affluent will *pay more*, but they are big sticklers for value.

As Jack recounted this story, he described how Judy initially played hard-ball with him. She felt violated, taken advantage of, and was determined not to let it happen again. Over the course of three separate meetings, Judy inquired about the number of clients Jack worked with, the level of service he provided, whether or not he would have time for her, how often he planned to meet with her, and finally, the details of his fee structure. Not once did she discuss the performance of her portfolio. In fact, Jack's advice was to leave everything in-place for now and develop a comprehensive financial plan that could serve as a road map for her.

Was this a bizarre anomaly? Perhaps. But selling to the affluent is full of anomalies. What the affluent have in common is that they earn more, have more cash to spend, and will pay you more in commissions and fees to get what they want. For those of you who understand how the affluent think, they are your treasure chest.

BMW, the German manufacturer of the "ultimate driving machine" has its pulse on the affluent consumer. Because BMW had always prided itself on being on the cutting edge of automobile performance and luxury, it tended to get ranked lower than competitors by various ratings organizations. Over time, BMW also developed a reputation for making high-maintenance automobiles. The inconvenience and expense of continually bringing their BMWs to the dealer for repairs was beginning to have an impact on affluent word-of-mouth decision making.

So, BMW changed. Not only did the car maker work feverishly to improve dependability, it unveiled the most comprehensive warranty program in the industry. At a time when Lexus was quietly scaling back its warranty service package, BMW rolled out a policy which (basically) states that you, the affluent BMW consumer, will have NO service charges for the first four years or 50,000 miles after buying your new automobile. Whether you need a routine oil change or replacement of a defective part, BMW says, "We are so confident in our product that we will stand behind it—come what may."

Like any product or service provider hoping to successfully market to the affluent, BMW continues to learn and adapt. The company now offers a form of tire insurance on high-performance tires and wheels. In *The Art of Selling to the Affluent,* I wrote about an affluent business owner who returned his wife's two-seat, high-performance Z after getting two flat tires within two weeks. At the time, BMW didn't keep these high-performance tires in stock, and didn't communicate their risks/benefits. The benefits included being able to corner at high speeds like a Grand-Prix race car driver. The risks were that the tires were easily punctured, didn't last as long, could not be repaired when punctured, were expensive to replace, and would ruin the high-performance wheels if they were driven for any distance while flat. Therefore, BMW launched a campaign to clearly communicate the risks/benefits of the tires and introduce a relatively inexpensive insurance package covering both tires and wheels.

This case history offers a number of lessons on marketing to the affluent. First, warranties and performance are statistically significant when trying to influence affluent word-of mouth. Second, price is not statistically significant. I bought the BMW with high-performance tires, and also purchased the optional tire insurance. I didn't want the high-performance package, but it was the only car of its model left, and I didn't want to wait for one to be shipped from Germany. So, I spent more for the high-performance package, once the tire risks/benefits were clearly communicated, and then opted for the protection.

Because the state of customer service in this country has deteriorated to the point where many consumers expect (and accept) poor treatment, *Caveat Emptor* seems to rule the land. Lots of people are happy when a business merely honors its promises—never mind exceeding expectations. But this doesn't apply to the affluent, and BMW is just one example of a company that understands this. The affluent demand nothing less than superior service, attention to detail, and hassle-free problem resolution, *and they are willing to pay* for these "privileges." The average person may be willing to spend hours on your customer-service or tech-support hotline. The affluent won't even bother to dial the number.

Research Facts

- Many of America's affluent don't believe they are rich until they've acquired $2.5 million in wealth.
- The Gen-X wealthy view the responsibility for their financial futures as being squarely and heavily on their shoulders.
- Most of today's affluent are "worker bees" who clock 50+ hours per week on the job.
- Upscale consumers often share the same attitudes, aspirations and—sometimes—purchasing habits of their wealthier neighbors, but they don't have the income and/or assets to qualify as affluent.

3

The "Doubting Thomas"

Affluent consumers with large families who were frequent shoppers [have] a greater propensity to report dissatisfaction with purchases than typical consumers.

—from *The Affluent Consumer*

Because the affluent are savvy, educated, and represent 39% of all consumer spending in this country, they have learned a great deal from their vast purchasing experiences. They are skeptical, don't believe advertising promises at face value, and are less likely to fall for celebrity endorsements (with athletic and fitness supplies a notable exception). They've been burned before, and will do their best to avoid repeating the same mistakes.

According to our APD Research,[15] when deciding *where* to look for options, survey respondents gave the highest credibility to opinions and suggestions from their immediate family and trusted friends. Our research and coaching experience also confirms that affluent consumers *do not* respond well to direct mail and telemarketing.

For service professionals, the prospecting methods that produce the greatest impact are targeted networking, referrals and introductions. To succeed, these activities require that you develop strong personal relationships with affluent prospects and clients. And you do this

---

[15] APD Research refers to *How the Affluent Make Purchasing Decisions*, commissioned by the Oechsli Institute, June 2004.

by attending or arranging live, real-time, in-person encounters—as many as it takes. In many ways, it's like a romance: you have to been seen, let your target get to know you, and then carefully let your intentions become known.

You can't buy affluent business *solely* with slick brochures, websites or direct-mail campaigns. You won't land them with hype, vague "value propositions" or "platinum-level" packages. You won't get their business unless they see genuine value in what you have to offer. You have to provide Ritz-Carlton service with FedEx efficiency. You have to be the *real deal.* On a consistent basis, in a myriad of ways, you must be able to quantify, demonstrate and communicate your value.

If you want to win business from the affluent, first win their confidence. *They must come to like you, trust you, and respect you as a professional—period!*

Hoisted by His Own Petard

A veteran real estate agent, Larry enjoyed a healthy income, belonged to a local country club, and drove a Lexus LS 460. In an attempt to list more luxury homes and project the right image, Larry worked with an advertising agency to create "a beautiful $20,000 electronic brochure" in the form of a website. But initially, this website cost him business.

The new website *was* beautiful. It described how he could provide every service a luxury homebuyer or seller could imagine. It also provided virtual tours of the homes he was listing. He wanted to communicate that he offered something very special, and couldn't wait for the site to begin generating traffic.

Larry acquired the listing of a prestigious physician who was interested in a new high-end condominium complex. In less than a week, however, Larry was embroiled in a conflict with this physician. Apparently, Larry neglected to inform the new client that he was leaving town on a 10-day cruise—a major faux-pas! His client wasn't pleased with what he considered "gross negligence," and insisted on pulling the listing.

Larry failed to understand that *HE* was the product that had to be sold, not a virtual tour. Although the site caught the attention of the physician, Larry soon found himself fighting to protect his reputation among the country-club set, of which this physician was an influential member. In fact, the physician's threat of negative word-of-mouth prompted Larry to relinquish the listing.

Larry learned the hard way that the affluent look beyond image, beyond gimmicks and beyond flash. Their focus is on substance. There was nothing wrong with Larry investing in a high-end website. The Internet is a major research tool for the affluent. What Larry learned was that this new marketing venue creates higher expectations among prospects, and demands a higher-level of commitment from the seller. Bottom line, *you must be as advertised!*

Personalized Service is a Must

Despite their middle-class self-image, the affluent demand highly personalized service, and expect high-priced service professionals to build relationships with them.

Most service professionals know what they must do to acquire, service and retain affluent clients. They spend millions saying so in their advertising. But advertising raises expectations, and our survey respondents sent a clear message about that: To secure our long-term business, *you must walk the talk* by becoming fully competent in providing solutions. You must deliver value by offering the necessary range of services.

Larry's client terminated his listing for two important reasons. First of all, by Larry's admission, the client had not been informed that he would be out-of-town on a 10-day cruise. Larry thought his new website would pave the way for him in the luxury home market and that his clientele would view him differently. But it took just a few days for his first online-generated affluent client to determine otherwise. Needless to say, Larry not only lost income, but even if he's able to stem the tide of negative word-of-mouth influence, he has lost a valuable source of introductions and referrals.

Of all the findings from our APD Research, the most surprising was our respondents' intense skepticism toward basic sales and marketing techniques—especially when it comes to intangibles (services). Another surprising result was their level of consumer savvy. You might think people with high disposable incomes would conduct less research—and would be less discerning—since they can "afford" to make mistakes. The opposite is true. The affluent are *more* discerning, because they've really learned from past mistakes. But as crusty and defensive as these wealthy prospects can be, *they will do almost anything for you once you prove yourself*—once you break down the barriers and develop a relationship based on mutual trust and professional respect.

> The affluent demand more and higher-quality services. Services, unlike physical products, are intangible and are not seen before purchased. The consumer getting advice must envision the outcome. For example, Pinnacle Care International of Baltimore charges members between $5,000 and $25,000 a year to maintain medical records, coordinate health care, and obtain speedy appointments with overbooked specialists. Since services are intangible, consumers try to discern evidence of quality in order to reduce risk.[16]

Spreading the Word

The affluent want more choices. But because we live in a world with a nearly infinite number of products and services from which to choose, top income earners insist on becoming well informed before making purchase decisions. On the surface, this poses a seeming dichotomy: wealthy Americans are usually pressed for time, and place a premium on time-saving products and services, but most are also willing to *take time* to conduct extensive research before buying—often via the Internet. But then, they're more likely to make the *actual purchase*, not online, but by visiting a physical retailer.

I said "seeming dichotomy," because—though the affluent value

[16] Michman, Ronald D. and Mazze, Edward M., *The Affluent Consumer*, p. 43.

time—they also value the experiential pleasures of receiving the kind of personalized service offered by the nation's foremost retailers.

> Luxury ultimately does not reside in the object, the product, the brand. Luxury is about the consumers' experience of it. So luxury is no longer a noun but a verb connoting the action and the delivery of the luxury experience and feeling to the consumer. . . .
>
> In understanding luxury from the perspective of consumers, luxury marketers must . . . look at their products not as the wonderful, beautiful, luxurious things they are but as the delivery mechanism through which they transmit a luxury experience to the consumer. The luxury marketer's challenge is to maximize the way the consumer experiences the luxury.[17]

In addition to valuing companies that provide high-quality products and better shopping experiences, the affluent look to companies that supply useful information for making purchases, especially on the Internet. Again, wealthy consumers tend to gather information on the Web, but they buy from physical retailers.

As avid Internet users, affluent consumers often conduct extensive online searches for the best mix of products, services, features, options and fees. If you haven't launched your own website yet, consider doing so *very* soon. But don't launch a site just because it seems fashionable, or because many of your competitors are doing so. Either do it right, or don't do it at all.

Many of the world's 36 million websites are resting peacefully in the Internet graveyard. They are nothing more than online billboards, brochures or catalogs that feature lists of products, value propositions and testimonials. They are rarely visited, and if they are, most visitors leave after about 10 seconds, never to return. Your site needs to offer more than that. The purpose of having a website is to pull targeted visitors toward the point of sale. As high-end product and service

[17] Danziger, Pamela N. *Let Them Eat Cake: Marketing Luxury to the Masses—as Well as the Classes*, p. 27.

providers, you may not make many sales based solely on your site's copy and design, but you can go a long way toward helping affluent customers clearly understand who you are, what you offer, and why you are superior to your rivals.

To attract affluent visitors, you must ensure that your site is easy to find, and easy to navigate. Your site must offer compelling reasons for prospects to fully explore your positioning, prices, products and services. Everything—absolutely everything—begins with selecting the right keywords and phrases. These keywords and phrases help you:

- Define your unique Internet niche and describe your business to others.
- Describe what you offer in terms of how your products and services provide value and solutions for your clients.
- Create a logo and tag line that immediately convince visitors that they've come to the right place.
- Help you decide how to organize your site so that targeted visitors can easily determine where they want to go next.
- Create titles, headings and content that relates to the interests and needs of targeted visitors.

Most important, you must choose appropriate keywords and phrases to help potential visitors actually find your site, and find it quickly—before they decide to browse your competitors' sites instead. If you've ever searched for a product or service provider in your region—from plumbers and house painters to accountants and attorneys—you know that search results often turn up hundreds, even thousands, of pages listing related websites. If you're like the vast majority of Web surfers, you'll only browse through the first page or so of the results to find what you want, leaving the sites on subsequent pages to languish in obscurity.

Life after the Sale

Most of today's affluent are willing to spend generously on time-saving and experience-enhancing goods and services. What's more, brand-name and status-enhancing items tend to be less important than the experiences and emotional impact that certain goods and services can deliver. Smart phones, Blackberrys, i-Phones, I-Pods, Wi-Fi Access, Broadband access, cable, cell phones for every member of the family, pet sitting services, dog walking services, lawn care, home cleaning, and high-level home security systems connected to Plasma TVs are just some items that meet these criteria.

The top quintile is very discriminating—the product or service better be as advertised or as promised. They want all the creature comforts they can afford, and are always looking to upgrade (get the better creature comfort). Advertising and marketing to this segment is a tricky business and must be done very carefully. The campaign must contain no false promises, yet be appealing enough to catch their attention. They shop for discounts (or like to think they're shopping for the best deals), but discounting doesn't impact their loyalty. Performance, service, and problem solving does.

NOTHING is more important than ensuring that your affluent customers are satisfied—not just at the moment of purchase but forever afterwards.

Too many sellers "drop the ball" once the customer has been "hooked," forgetting that a customer's subsequent satisfaction or dissatisfaction will greatly influence his purchasing behavior in the future. Not only that, it will also determine whether your business generates positive word-of-mouth among the client's influential friends, family and business associates.

When deciding whether to use the same service provider again, our APD respondents gave the strongest influence to:

- Any problems I encountered were resolved quickly and satisfactorily.
- They provided good service following my purchase.
- They previously provided information I needed to make a satisfactory decision.

Selling to the affluent goes well beyond making the sale—though you *do* have to make the sale. It requires you to solve problems quickly and satisfactorily, and deliver superior service following the purchase.

Harold and Maude offer a perfect illustration of this point[18].

After building a nest egg worth more than $250,000, Harold—a small business owner—and his wife Maude pursued their dream of living in the country. Life looked like "Green Acres" until tax time arrived.

Normally, Harold filed the family's tax returns using a popular software package. Because of the volume of financial transactions related to the move and a recent inheritance, Harold thought it wise to hire an accountant. He queried his mother-in-law, who lived nearby, as well as several neighbors for a referral. One name popped up again and again—that of John.

Harold telephoned John, and was greeted with a warm hello and thanks to those who'd referred him. At their first meeting, John impressed Harold with his requests for detailed information and the fact that he prepared returns for the town's most prominent families. Harold was sold.

Six weeks after handing over his financial data, however, Harold hadn't heard back from John. Two telephone messages went unanswered. Eight weeks later, John finally called to inform Harold that the returns were ready. Harold picked up the returns, wrote a check to John, and discussed potential future assignments. However, when Maude arrived home that evening, she discovered that John had failed to prepare a New York State and City return. Harold called to complain, but hung up when he was connected to voicemail. That night, he bought a copy of Turbo-Tax, and prepared the missing returns himself.

You might think Harold acted hastily by not giving John a chance to correct his mistake and/or by paying for services not rendered. In fact, Harold's behavior was typical of affluent consumers—he demanded that the job be done quickly, correctly and with a minimum of fuss. When it became obvious that he'd "picked the wrong horse," he didn't waste more valuable time, and he finished "the race" himself. Like many self-made men and women, Harold had neither the time nor the patience for shoddy service.

---

[18] A real couple, but I've (obviously) changed their names.

A Challenging, Changing Market

If there's one thing that's always defined baby boomers, including the affluent, it's their desire for change and improvement. Their penchant for transforming American society is less radical than during the '60s and '70s, but continues to pose challenges to businesses and governments alike. First and foremost, you cannot count on boomers and Gen-Xers to behave like their parents and grandparents.

Although the affluent were once the stalwarts of the Republicans party, for example, political affiliations are becoming more blurred—in part because many younger affluent have been "turned off" by the war in Iraq, and the perceived fiscal irresponsibility, lack of competence and partisan politics of the last half decade. Another factor is their middle-class roots. For a variety of reasons, today's affluent boomers tend to be fiscally conservative but more socially engaged than old-school Republicans, possibly because they don't consider themselves wealthy. On the other hand, they don't care for their 79% tax bite, and—like their older peers—are always looking for ways to minimize this burden.

The younger affluent may be economically conservative, but they are more socially responsible than older generations of the wealthy. This helps explain the increasing popularity of "green" products and services among the affluent, since—after all—it was the boomers who pioneered the environmental movement in the first place.

Affluent boomers now control serious money—more than many ever expected to acquire, and they buy a lot of products and services. These goods and services must constantly evolve, however, to keep pace with their needs and wants. Top quintile members are early adopters, want personalized service and do their comparison-shopping homework.

Since maturing boomers are the wealthiest generation in history, with so much money in (or about to be in) transition, understanding their psychographic profile is a must. As I mentioned in the introduction, the most recent research findings have allowed us to develop *Four Key Affluent Motivators for Life's Decision Making:*

✓ Personal Health
✓ Family Health
✓ Financial Health
✓ Spiritual Health

In short order, you'll discover how these key motivators are closely associated, and in many instances overlap. Because a growing number of affluent boomers are entering their prime earning years—i.e., "aging"—and are self-absorbed, I'll begin with what's most upfront and personal to them: *personal health.*

Research Facts

- Affluent consumers with large families who were frequent shoppers had a greater propensity to report dissatisfaction with purchases than typical consumers.
- When deciding whether to use the same service provider again, our APD respondents gave the strongest influence to:

  —Any problems I encountered were resolved quickly and satisfactorily.
  —They provided good service following my purchase.
  —They provided information I needed to make a satisfactory decision.
- The affluent tend to perform research online, but actually purchase from the physical retailer.
- Most of today's affluent are willing to spend generously on time-saving and experience-enhancing goods and services.

SECTION II

4 Key Affluent Motivators

4

Personal Health

Only 25% of affluent investors currently own a long-term care insurance policy.

—Citigroup Smith Barney Affluent Investor Poll, April 2006

Are you concerned about your health? How's your blood pressure? How about your cholesterol? Could you drop a few pounds? Do you belong to a health club or own exercise equipment? Do you feel a bit arthritic when you wake-up? Do you take Ibuprofen? How's your eyesight? Have you had any "sun-spots" removed? Have you considered Botox? I could go on, but you get the idea. If your answer is "Yes" to any of the above, welcome to the dichotomous world of affluent boomers!

You might not think so at first glance, but *personal health* is a strong motivator for affluent decision making. (I realize, however, that an objective observer strolling through a major airport, supermarket, or food court would conclude otherwise.) People are getting bigger in the wrong places because they eat too much, exercise too little, and eat too many of the wrong foods. Yet personal health is a key motivator.

Therefore, an entire industry has grown up around the bizarre relationship between how we currently look, how we want to look, and personal health. Care to take a guess at the fastest-growing sun-care product? Hint: it's not sunscreen. The prize goes to self-tanners. Sales of spray-on tanners have skyrocketed since the turn of the century, coinciding with the number of affluent boomers who are starting to have pieces of their sun-damaged skin removed.

If you've traveled to California recently, you might have noticed that nobody is smoking in public places. There are even no-smoking signs on sidewalks by the pier in Santa Monica. I live in North Carolina, the tobacco capital of the world, and there is a no-smoking ordinance here (though not as stringent as in California). How do you think this legislation got passed? By affluent boomers, many of whom quit smoking, and now recognize that the Surgeon General was right to claim that smoking is the chief preventable cause of death in our society. Personal health is a strong motivator.

Circling back to the sun issue, New York and New Jersey have just passed laws banning children under 14 from using tanning parlors. Some analysts are predicting that indoor tanning will soon begin feel serious regulatory pressure from federal agencies.

This is not to presume that affluent boomers are a bunch of health nuts. It would be much too easy to understand them if their attitudes and habits were that homogenous. We are living longer than our ancestors, but much of that can be attributed to advances in medicine and elder care. In many ways, affluent boomers are a walking-talking contradiction: they want the best of both worlds.

If you work with the affluent—or plan to—you should possess a thorough understanding of their idiosyncrasies. This translates into understanding their "psychographics"—the analysis of a specific market segment based on its values, attitudes, interests and lifestyles.

Since the dawn of civilization, the wealthiest citizens have spent generously in order to obtain better health care facilities, personal physicians, and to visit spas and resorts featuring everything from "healing waters" to the latest fads in nutrition and exercise. For example, breakfast magnate C.W. Post was inspired to create his own cereal business after sampling the menu at a sanitarium founded by Corn Flakes inventor John Harvey Kellogg.

Unlike their near and distant ancestors, however, today's affluent are assuming greater personal responsibility for their own appearance, physical fitness and health.

Not so long ago, most affluent baby boomers had only a vague understanding of terms such as systolic and diastolic, triglycerides and cholesterol. Today, most can recite their cholesterol and blood pressure stats like a baseball fan rattling off the batting averages of favorite players. These boomers also know the difference between "good" and "bad" cholesterol, and how lifestyle choices impact their overall health.

If anyone has doubts that *personal health* has become a major motivator for America's top quintile income earners, they need look no farther than the sound bites of politicians running for higher office. Regardless of party affiliation, health care has become a common theme in their rhetoric. Three former presidents (George H.W. Bush, Jimmy Carter and Gerald Ford) have served—or currently serve—as honorary co-chairmen of the National Coalition on Health Care, and are front and center in the recent report, *Building a Better Health Care System.* Protestations to the contrary, political pressure isn't building because our esteemed politicians have suddenly acquired a bleeding heart for the downtrodden of society.

So what's the motivation behind the focus on health care? The reason is the affluent—that huge and influential group of aging, affluent baby-boomers. Many are business owners and self-employed professionals. Some work in the medical world, others are executives, and others are retired or soon-to-be retired—all of whom have experienced escalating health care costs. You don't have to be an economist to recognize a serious problem when the average annual premiums for employer-sponsored family health coverage jump from $7,053 in 2001 to $14,563 in 2006.[19]

As the cost of health care (personal health) rises, everyone feels the pinch. Many of today's top quintile have elderly parents, and many also have first-hand experience dealing with the spiraling cost of prescription drugs.

My Saturday morning tennis group is a perfect example of the idiosyncratic relationship that affluent boomers have with personal health. Composed of doctors, attorneys and UNC professors, everyone qualifies as an aging affluent boomer, and everyone would take issue

[19] *Building a Better Health Care System; Specifications for Reform,* National Coalition on Health Care, 2004.

with my use of "affluent" to describe them. Personal health is always the first and last topic of our Saturday morning tennis discussions.

Our personal health issues include: two knee replacements; one neck surgery; one back surgery; countless knee operations requiring braces; seven of 10 members taking statins; one member taking nerve blockers, so he can play tennis without his arm going numb from a disc problem in his neck; everyone carrying a personal supply of Ibuprofen and ice packs; approximately three-quarters of the group exercising consistently; and someone always being on a diet. And this is a group that, compared to most Americans in the same demographic category, is considered fit and athletic!

The time, money and energy expended in our attempts to defy aging are mind boggling when viewed from a distance. But these efforts make perfect sense from a personal perspective.

Like other income quintiles, affluent Americans still eat too much and exercise too little. But unlike the other quintiles, wealthy citizens are trying harder—and largely succeeding—in maintaining better appearances and staying healthier. Like my tennis group, they spend more money on spas, fitness centers, vitamins and health-food products, and both women and men are undergoing surgery to make them look more youthful.

A Pound of Prevention

An increasing number of the affluent are hiring personal cooks or catering services to serve nutritious foods in their homes, and many are employing personal fitness trainers. The personal trainer industry is experiencing a huge surge in demand, with the U.S. Department of Labor forecasting a 50% growth rate through the next decade. Meanwhile, gyms and fitness centers are targeting aging baby boomers with marketing campaigns designed to appeal to those who might feel uncomfortable exercising next to "Greek Gods" and Supermodels.

> People over 55 now represent nearly a quarter of all health club members, according to the International Health, Racquet and

Sportsclub Association. The increase has been the defining change in the fitness center industry over the past 15 years.

Gyms that vied for the youth market with snazzy juice bars and tanning salons now offer low-impact courses like water aerobics, walking, or chair aerobics, which aren't so tough on the joints. Even major chains are lowering the adrenaline to make seniors feel at ease.[20]

Overall, Americans spent $4.3 billion on exercise equipment in 2002, up more than 11% from the previous year. Treadmills, the most popular category of home exercise equipment, are the biggest hit with 45- to 65-year-olds, who were responsible for 44% of this $2.5 billion market in 2002. Some of the affluent are spending $12,000+ to equip in-home fitness centers with the latest exercise machines.[21] Of course, much of that equipment ends up gathering dust after a few months, unless exercise enthusiasts are particularly motivated or have personal trainers to ensure they remain motivated, but that's a subject for another book.

According to a Gallup Poll, it appears people are aware of the amount of time they actually spend exercising. And it seems most of us could "kick it up a notch."

Perception of Exercising:

- 59.25%—I spend too little time exercising
- 36.77%—I spend about the right amount of time exercising
- 2.74%—I spend too much time exercising

2005 Gallup Poll

Once again, we enter the dichotomous realm of affluent boomers. Although Gallup indicates that nearly two-thirds of those polled admit

[20] "Gyms Running After Baby Boomers—and Those Older." Associated Press, September 3, 2005, as reprinted by www.azcentral/com.

[21] Louise Chu, "Fitness Rush: Creating Their Own Gyms at Home." Associated Press, February, 17, 2004.

they spend too little time exercising, aging affluent boomers continue to buy exercise equipment, spa memberships and all of the accompanying paraphernalia.

> The number of spas has more than doubled to over 12,000 from 1997 to 2003, with revenue accounting for $11.2 billion in 2003. Luxury product marketers, personal-care companies, and private-equity firms are all endeavoring to serve other growing markets. Firms such as Starwood Hotels and Resorts Worldwide Inc, North Castle, which purchased Elizabeth Arden, and Mario Tricoci have entered this lucrative market. Among the services offered by these spas are hairstylists and pedicures.
>
> Upscale salons and spas are developing strategies toward the lucrative men's market. Men currently account for over 20 percent of spa visits according to the International Spa Association and marketers desire to attract more males in the future. Strategies include decorating in warm, earthy colors; hiring both male and female therapists; and offering special classes such as golf clinics or sessions with exercise consultants. Privacy is essential for men. The best way to reach men is through a wife or girlfriend who has purchased a gift certificate for them. Print ads are also helpful.[22]

And while we're at it, let's not forget the health and fitness needs of the four-legged members of affluent households. This is another prime example of why aging boomers often are considered, as one of our statisticians put it, "nuttier than a fruitcake." Draw your own conclusions from the following, but one thing is certain: the affluent spend money.

> Expenditures on pet health are increasing. Health therapies such as CAT scans [no pun intended] and MRIs, kidney transplants, root canals, and chemotherapy treatments once reserved for people are now extended to pets.[23]

---

[22] Michman, Ronald D. and Mazze, Edward M., *The Affluent Consumer,* p. 152.
[23] Ibid., p. 149.

"Boutique Medicine"

With apologies to the MDs in my tennis group, survey after survey has shown that the majority of Americans are dissatisfied with the medical care they receive—in terms of quality, level of personal attention and access to personal physicians when and where needed. Such complaints are at the center of today's public-policy arguments about how to reform the nation's health care system. Some of the affluent, however, are taking advantage of a fairly new option—known as "concierge," "retainer" or "boutique" medicine.

These medical practices accept limited numbers of patients and offer increased levels of service. Typical boutique services include unlimited access to a physician at any time (day or night), immediate access appointments, research on complex or rare diseases, coordination of care with specialists, guidance through a hospitalization, complex executive physicals, and other amenities designed to appeal to wealthy clientele.

For this level of service, practices charge hefty prices, as high as $10,000+ per year. Boutique practice physicians are said to reap such benefits as the opportunity to care for fewer patients with longer visits and less paperwork. Instead of a typical panel of 2,000 to 3,000 patients, each physician may care for as few as 400 patients.

> Anyone searching the country for a group of patients who are perfectly happy with their medical care, neither brutalized by the system nor fearful that the onset of a serious illness will plunge them into a morass of confusion and neglect, need look no farther than Dr. Kaminetsky's waiting room here in Boca Raton.
>
> Not that the waiting room usually has anyone in it. One promise made to patients paying for concierge service is that waiting will not be a part of their health care experience. Patients are guaranteed that phone calls will be returned promptly, appointments will be scheduled on a same-day basis if necessary, and appointment times will be honored. A bowl of fruit salad and platters of bagels and sponge cake set out for

> patients in the waiting room can go barely touched over the course of a day, and the television often plays to an empty couch.
>
> A relatively simple tradeoff is responsible: the extra fees collected from patients let concierge doctors, who leave regular practice for concierge medicine, slash their caseloads. Before Dr. Kaminetsky became a concierge doctor five years ago he had 2,500 patients in his practice—a standard number for most primary care internists. His list now numbers 600.
>
> Sick and well alike, patients are delighted with the results.
>
> Joan Holzman, 69, takes no medicines and has no health problems; she comes to the office once a year for a physical exam, an X-ray, an electrocardiogram and blood tests. "I adore it," Ms. Holzman said. "Before, wherever you went you felt like cattle. But everyone here is top-notch—the doctors, the secretaries, the nurses. They're warm, like family. It's a wonderful feeling of security."[24]

From my perspective, this is only the tip of the iceberg for boutique medical clinics. The aging affluent boomer has the means and the desire to get high-quality medical care, so this medical niche will continue to be a growth industry as affluent boomers keep aging.

Concerns over Rising Costs

Despite the satisfaction of "boutique" patients with the quality of care and personalized attention—always priorities for the affluent, regardless of what they're purchasing—the vast majority of the affluent feel anything but secure about the rapidly increasing cost of health care. Like everyone else, much of the top quintile feels vulnerable to how a catastrophic or long-term illness might affect family finances. And anyone who recalls Economics 101 recognizes that the demand for health

---

[24] Abigail Zuger, "For a Retainer, Lavish Care by 'Boutique Doctors.'" *The New York Times*, October 30, 2005.

care is "inelastic"—i.e., something so critical that people aren't going to stop taking their insulin just because the price went up.

According to a 2006 Citigroup Smith Barney poll, the cost of health care is a major concern for affluent investors, more so than the quality of care available. The issues of greatest concern are the cost of prescription drugs, health insurance and long-term care (with about 50% of respondents being very concerned about these issues). Only 25% expressed strong concern about quality of care offered by doctors or hospitals.

These investors blamed problems with the nation's health care system on health insurance companies, pharmaceutical companies, lawyers and the federal government, with the largest numbers naming attorneys and the federal government as most responsible. What was interesting to note was that the greater the person's wealth, the more likely he was to blame lawyers as major contributors to problems in the health care system.

Vast majorities would support *any* change to the current system, with most saying they strongly favored malpractice limits (56%), allowing small companies and individuals to join together to purchase health insurance at better group rates (69%), and allowing low- and middle-income workers to deduct the cost of health-insurance premiums from their taxes (50%). Nearly 50% favored easing restrictions on imported prescription drugs and establishing tax incentives for those with high-deductible plans.

Personal Health Concerns

According to the survey, "One reason that health care costs are a top-of-mind issue for affluent investors may be the fact that eight out of ten have seen their health insurance costs increase over the past year. In addition, their personal health is something very important to these investors. When asked to rank the importance of various areas in their life, investors place their health second, on average, behind family, but far ahead of financial security or career. They also back-up the importance of health with their pocketbook, as more than half report that they make donations to non-profit organizations that focus on health issues.

"One of the health issues that concerns investors the most is the idea of becoming ill or injured and requiring long-term nursing home care. More than one-quarter of affluent investors describe themselves as very concerned about this possibility; nearly as many are very concerned about the possibility of becoming disabled. A majority of affluent investors say that their concerns about each of these have increased over the past year.

"When investors think about their retirement years, seven in ten are at least somewhat concerned about being able to pay the cost of long-term care, either in a nursing home or at home. Likewise, seven in ten have concerns about outliving the money they have saved for retirement, and even more are at least somewhat concerned about maintaining their desired standard of living throughout retirement (eight in ten).

Despite their concerns regarding the potential cost of long-term care and the fact that more than half believe that they are likely to need long-term care assistance at some point in their life, *most of these investors have not done any planning for their own long-term care needs* [emphasis added]. Only 25% of affluent investors currently own a long-term care insurance policy. As might be expected, ownership of long-term care policies is more common among the *more affluent* (34% among those with assets of $500,000 or more).

"One in three overall have at least discussed the idea of long-term care insurance with their financial advisor, although in many cases those who had such a discussion elected not to purchase a policy (often deciding that it was not a good investment).

"Concerns about health and medical costs in old age are related to the fact that many affluent investors have personal experience dealing with the needs of the elderly. Seven out of ten have personally known someone who has needed long-term care assistance, and four in ten say that either they or their spouse have provided hands-on care or other types of assistance to an elderly parent or relative. Those who have been through this experience are among the most likely to report being concerned about having to live in a nursing home or having to depend on others to care for them. However, these concerns have not led to increased ownership of long-term care insurance among this group."[25]

Once again, the idiosyncratic relationship between affluent boomers and personal health is on full display. They recognize the need, many have first-hand experience in caring for parents, they have the resources, but on a personal level the issues are often out-of-sight, out-of-mind until some time in the distant future.

I'd be remiss if I didn't mention another factor regarding this topic. The affluent do not like salespeople, and tend to view insurance agents as salespeople. This is why insurance agents must work that much harder to re-brand themselves. They should also, like anyone attempting to market their products and services to this market, master the art of selling to the affluent.

Opportunities

The information above should serve as a wake-up call for most members of the financial services profession—especially insurance providers—as well as those engaged in providing nutrition, fitness, medical and nursing services. Affluent Americans are extremely concerned about their personal health and that of family members, and are willing to spend billions of dollars to maintain or improve their overall appearance, physical fitness, and to secure high-quality medical care. But, though many of these people are concerned about rising costs and the potential impact of long-term illnesses on their finances, few are *actively* pursuing long-term care insurance or making plans to cope with health problems as they reach retirement and beyond. The opportunities are mind blowing for those who come to understand, and correctly market, to the affluent.

So, in the spirit of personal health . . . When was the last time you stepped on a scale? Were you pleased with your reading? If not, what

[25]Citigroup Smith Barney Affluent Investor Poll, April 3 and April 18, 2006, as reported by http://www.advisorpage.com.

are you doing about it? How many prescriptions are you currently taking? Do you feel healthier? How many days did you exercise last week? Are you pleased with your fitness routine? Did you emphasize health and fitness, in some form or fashion, to a family member over the past week?

Nothing will trigger personal health motivators more than being forced to answer personal health questions. And aging affluent boomers are being asked these questions, in some shape and form on a regular basis. Their responses are impacting the decisions they are making.

By now, you have most likely made the connection between personal health and family health. As I've previously indicated, to fully understand today's affluent, it is important to recognize how these key motivators are linked. After all, each is critical to their decision making. And decision making for the affluent usually signals money in motion.

Research Facts

- The Department of Labor forecasts a 50% growth rate for personal trainers through the next decade.
- People over 55 now represent nearly a quarter of all health club members.
- The number of spas more than doubled to over 12,000 from 1997 to 2003, with revenue accounting for $11.2 billion.
- The cost of health care is a major concern for affluent investors, more so than the quality of care available.
- Only 25% of affluent investors currently own a long-term care insurance policy.

5

Family Health

Funding their children's college education is a low financial priority for the affluent.

—2007 "Understanding the Affluent" research study

Anyone hoping to understand the affluent American family must understand—first and foremost—that the average top-quintile family is headed by two parents of different sexes who are both college educated and, between them, earn an average household income of $132,000. That's a given. However . . .

Although the family unit of today's top-quintile wage earners is an extremely important motivator, it's changing. Television shows like *Father Knows Best* and *Ozzie and Harriet* reflected the family unit at a time when over 75% of the population was married. According to the U.S. Census Bureau, today's figure is 59%, down from 72% in 1970. This changing family landscape is driven, in part, by the fact that approximately 50% of all first marriages end in divorce (U.S. Census Bureau 1997). What we're witnessing *and* experiencing is a changing definition, at least from the affluent viewpoint, of the family unit.

None of this is lost on American corporations, which spend over $15 billion annually on marketing to children, an increase from $6.2 billion in 1992.[26] The marketing industry recognizes the influence

[26] P.W. Lauro, "Coaxing the Smile that Sells: Baby Wranglers in Demand in Marketing for Children, *The New York Times*, November 1, 1999, p. C1.

children have on purchase decisions, small and large. By capitalizing on two factors of the changing family unit—two working parents, single/divorced parents—advertisers can blitz the average child with about 40,000 television commercials per year.[27] The impact of children on consumer spending is tremendous, with children influencing purchases that total more than $600 billion annually![28] Not only does this directly affect our prime affluent boomers' lifestyle, it is creating a "cornucopia generation" of insatiable consumers. As you can imagine, or know from first-hand experience, this impacts a family's *financial health.*

Young "cradle-to-grave" consumers (so named by Dr. Susan Linn, a psychologist at Judge Baker Children's Center and Harvard Medical School), of top-quintile families are *expected* to attend college—and most do. Many receive masters and post-graduate degrees. That's a given. The children of America's top income earners can't imagine that their offspring would do anything *but* attend premier universities here and abroad to acquire the best education money can buy. For these reasons, wealthy Americans don't invest much emotional energy worrying over funding their children's education. They *do* save for those educations, but then they stop worrying. Education, a good career, regular promotions, founding their own companies—these are all givens—like breathing, eating and sleeping.

For this reason, financial professionals should avoid investing too much emotional and intellectual energy trying to convince the affluent to plan for their children's college educations. According to our latest survey, this financial area is one of affluent America's lowest priorities—but keep in mind that it's the *planning* that's ranked low, not the actual saving.

---

[27] Kunkel, David D., as published in Singer, Dorothy G. and Singer, Jerome L. (Eds), *The Handbook of Children and the Media.* Thousand Oaks, CA: Sage Publications, 2000, p. 376.

[28] "The Kids Market," New York: MarketResearch.com. March 2000.

Marriage Breeds Success and Vice Versa

The news media has long pointed out the widening income gulf in American society, but only recently have sociologists and economists begun piecing together the correlation between marriage, education and income. What they have discovered is a widening gap between how affluent Americans approach marriage and child-rearing, and how the less affluent do. The overall conclusion is that traditional marriage generates more affluence, and this affluence perpetuates traditional marriages and then perpetuates continued affluence.

> Among the elite (excluding film stars), the nuclear family is holding up quite well. Only 4% of the children of mothers with college degrees are born out of wedlock. And the divorce rate among college-educated women has plummeted. Of those who first tied the knot between 1975 and 1979, 29% were divorced within ten years. Among those who first married between 1990 and 1994, only 16.5% were.
>
> At the bottom of the education scale, the picture is reversed. Among high-school dropouts, the divorce rate rose from 38% for those who first married in 1975–79 to 46% for those who first married in 1990–94. . . .
>
> Does this matter? Kay Hymowitz of the Manhattan Institute, a conservative think tank, says it does. In her book, "Marriage and Caste in America," she argues that the "marriage gap" is the chief source of the country's notorious and widening inequality. Middle-class kids growing up with two biological parents are "socialized for success." They do better in school, get better jobs and go onto create intact families of their own. Children of single parents or broken families do worse in school, get worse jobs and go on to have children out of wedlock. This makes it more likely that those born near the top or the bottom will stay where they started.
>
> A large majority—92%—of children whose families make more than $75,000 a year live with two parents (including

stepparents). At the bottom of the income scale . . . only 20% of children live with two parents. . . .

Marriage itself is a wealth-generating institution, according to Barbara Dafoe Whitehead and David Popenoe, who run the National Marriage Project at Rutgers University. Those who marry "till death do us part" end up, on average, four times richer than those who never marry. This is partly because marriage provides economies of scale—two can live more cheaply than one—and because the kind of people who make more money—those who work hard, plan for the future and have good interpersonal skills—are more likely to marry and stay married. . . .[29]

The Grand Ole Market

As convincing as these arguments are, there's more to creating and maintaining affluence in the changing American family. It's important to recognize that, though affluent boomers are remaining in their marriages in greater numbers than the rest of the population, more and more affluent children are being raised by a single parent, and more and more families are headed by *two* working parents. This means that affluent children are fending for themselves for longer periods of time. The stress, fear, guilt and spending—a potpourri of emotions linked to the actions of both children and parents—is having a big impact on *family health.* This leads us to another dynamic of today's affluent family.

Another reason affluent families become—and remain—well-to-do is attributable to the roles played by today's Silent Generation and boomer grandparents—those "doting seniors" with more money to spend on their grandchildren than ever before. Today's grandchildren are reaping the benefits of affluent older generations who intend to "spoil them rotten."

There are an estimated 80 million grandparents in the U.S. (on the

[29] "The Frayed Knot." *The Economist*, May 26–June 1, 2007, pgs. 24–25.

high side), ranging from 45 to 65, with each grandparent having an average of six grandchildren. A growing number of these grandmas and grandpas are baby boomers who account for 77% of the nation's wealth, and stand to inherit more wealth from their thrifty parents than any other generation in American history. For these reasons, grandparents currently spend $30 billion annually on their grandkids, "and the amount a grandparent spends on a grandchild increases as the grandchild gets older, possibly because older grandkids are going to college, buying houses and doing other things that require a lot of money."

> It's no surprise that grandparents are a great market for kids' products. Many grandparents take care of their grandkids at least part of the time, so they purchase cribs, strollers and other childcare products so that the child's parents don't have to transport these items to grandma's and grandpa's house. And . . . as of 2002 (the year in which the AARP's last grandparents survey was published), 4.5 million kids were living with their grandparents.
>
> The survey also reveals that 87 percent of grandparents buy clothing for their grandkids; 80 percent buy books; 76 percent purchase toys; and 45 percent give their grandkids videos and DVDs. Grandparents also help with day-to-day expenses, and many take their grandkids on trips as well.
>
> While grandparents spend a good deal of money on their grandkids, that doesn't mean they buy nothing for themselves! "They tend to buy automobiles, second homes, and exotic vacations or adventure vacations," [says Judy Awsumb, executive vice president of GRAND media]. "Grandparents account for 53 percent of all luxury travel." Anything that comes under the "travel" header, like rental cars and hotels, also are a good bet. Other important purchases for grandparents are insurance and financial products.
>
> Grandparents do respond well to direct mail, but don't discount online marketing as an effective way to reach them. "A

significant amount of marketing should be online—more than most marketers realize," says Michael Heaney, vice president of list brokerage at Specialists Marketing Services. "Grandparents are typically well-educated with respect to knowledge and technology. Grandparents are e-mailing their friends, children and grandchildren at least three to five times a week."

Since the majority of buying for grandkids (and for their households) is done by women, it's a good idea to target grandmothers in your marketing. "We have found targeting to women has increased response and improved overall performance," says Heaney.[30]

Second Homes and Retirement Homes

Unless you've been living in a cave for the past decade, you know that as the affluent reach their peak earning years, they purchase second and (sometimes) third homes. Until recently, many of these houses and condominiums were located in or near resort destinations along the coasts. Today, it's become nearly impossible to keep track of all of the burgeoning "hot spots" for second homes. An affluent family is as likely to own a vacation home in Montana, Michigan or the mountains of the Carolinas as in Long Island's Hamptons or Cape Cod.

Even in the midst of the current sub-prime debacle, the top quintile's appetite for second homes or their "dream" home to wile away their future days in retirement remains strong. This has created a booming business for tradesmen, professionals and various industries that serve these maturing baby-boomers.

For instance, our family's beach home needs a new deck, and the contractor we hired has only lived in the area for two years. He's already built a strong reputation, and built decks for two of our neighbors (word-of-mouth influence at work), but he learned his craft in

[30] Linda Formichelli, "Market Focus: Grandparents." *Target Marketing*, July 1, 2007. www.targetmarketingmag.com.

Massachusetts. When I asked what prompted him to move his family and his entire operation to North Carolina, he smiled, telling me that a friend in the building business said, "If you want to make a lot of money, get your a** down here and make money from all these people who have money." That's precisely what he's doing.

For many affluent boomers, *family health* centers on finances, as you can see in Chart 5-1 below. In other words, *financial health* is often equivalent to *family health.*

This financial focus becomes more pronounced when it's time for the affluent to retire. Florida no longer dominates the market for retirement relocation, as many of the older affluent seek to remain closer to friends and family (especially grandchildren). As of this writing, some of the "hot retirement spots" named by *The Wall Street Journal* and MSNBC include: Ashland, Oregon; San Antonio, Texas; New Bern and Mount Airy, North Carolina; St. George, Utah; and—overseas—Nicaragua, Honduras and Panama.

During the past decade, for example, many retirees from cities such as Baltimore, Washington, D.C., Philadelphia and New York have been

Chart 5-1

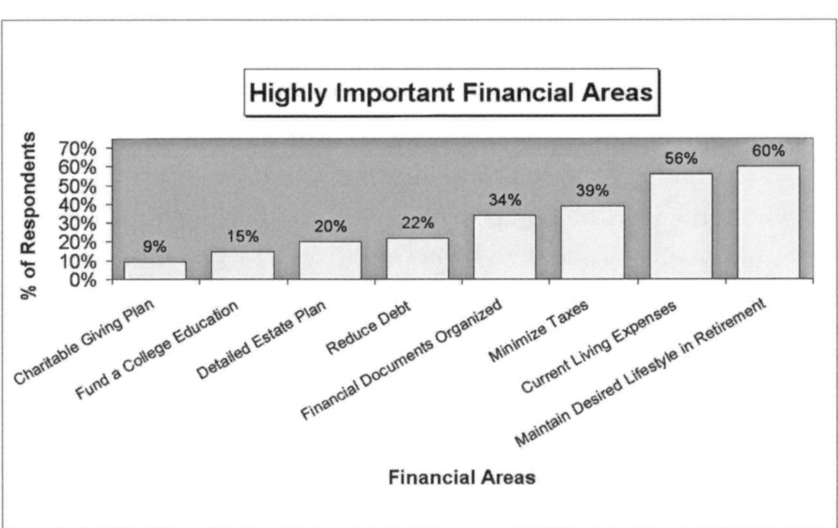

relocating to the eastern shores of Delaware, Maryland and Virginia (Delmarva), and purchasing homes worth $500,000+, thereby fueling a building boom that only slowed as the housing slump of 2006 took hold. The Carolinas, too, are undergoing a major real estate boom fueled by retirees with second homes located on the beach or in the mountains. As Phoenix reaches the limits of expansion, more retirees are looking to Las Vegas and locations in New Mexico. Affluent retirees want a luxurious lifestyle, access to health care, top-quality restaurants, golf courses, etc.—whether these are located near their second homes or their retirement homes.

But not all of the older affluent are buying condos located near the 18th hole of a retirement community overlooking the ocean. One of the hottest trends sees affluent retirees moving into luxury apartments in the revitalized downtowns of major cities such as New York and Chicago—not typical "Sunbelt" destinations. Affluent retirees who relocate to urban centers are seeking to enjoy a nearly endless list of museums, galleries, concerts and sporting events, and to free themselves from maintaining lawns or worrying that golf balls will crash through their windows at any moment.

In another trend, many of the *most* senior citizens are migrating back to the north—or at least halfway back.

> For the first time since the Depression, more Americans ages 75 and older have been leaving the South than moving there, according to a New York Times analysis of Census Bureau data.
>
> The reversal appears to be driven, in part by older people who retired to the South in their 60s, but decided to return home to their children and grandchildren in the Northeast, Midwest and West after losing spouses or becoming less mobile.
>
> A stream of elderly transplants leaving Florida was detected by sociologists two decades ago, including so-called half-backs, who stopped short of returning to their home states and settled elsewhere in the South. What is new is the growth in the

number of people leaving the region entirely and the dimension of the migration.[31]

Upscale Assisted Living

As noted in the previous chapter, the affluent are deeply concerned about the rising cost of health care, especially the potentially disastrous costs of long-term care. Yet relatively few actually take out insurance or make serious plans for themselves or parents. Despite this, a number of companies are anticipating demand for the kind of upscale living environments and health care services that the aging are likely to want.

Upscale assisted-living is a booming industry, and nowhere is this more apparent that in Charlotte, North Carolina, which is attracting an increasing number of large investments by companies specializing in state-of-the-art, upscale communities for older adults. Within the last three years, several companies have entered the Charlotte market, including: Manorhouse and Brighton by Marriott; Alterra (which operates 470 residences and 28 states); Atria, (with 9,100 communities in 26 states); and Sunrise Assisted Living (one of the nation's oldest providers of assisted living care, which operates 162 communities in 24 states). The phenomenal growth of upscale communities is catering to the growing population of more affluent retirees.

One example is the Cypress in south Charlotte, which features a grand ballroom, elegant dining, a fitness center, library and indoor swimming in a 40,000-square-foot clubhouse. This upscale retirement community is located on 60 acres and includes villas (apartments), cottages, a wellness center, and assisted living and skilled nursing beds. Such communities charge a one-time entrance fee in the neighborhood of $30,000 to $200,000 and a monthly fee ranging from $1,300 to $4,500+, depending on the services and facilities provided.

Thanks to affluent boomers, there is now a continuum of care.

---

[31] Sam Roberts, "Making the Return Trip: The Elderly Head North." *The New York Times*, February 26, 2007.

Fifty years ago, the only alternative to home care for the elderly was a nursing home. But as the 77 million boomers approach retirement age, they are demanding more and better for themselves and their parents. In 30 years, the number of Americans aged 85 and older will double to 8.5 million.

Chart 5-2

Very/Extremely Important	
Family	98%
Health	90%
Friends	79%
Leisure	67%
Money	65%
Religion	57%
Hobbies	53%

**2005 Gallup Polls*

Furry and Feathered Friends

The affluent American family comprises more than human beings. Like nearly every American family, the wealthy love and pamper their dogs, cats, birds, snakes, lizards, hamsters, etc. The major difference between the top quintile and everyone else is the degree to which the affluent are willing to care for their furry and feathered friends. Today, pets are routinely undergoing surgical procedures that were pioneered only a few decades ago to save the lives of humans. And, in addition to caring for their pets' physical well-being, many affluent are concerned with their animals' emotional needs.

As I was writing this chapter, we received a frantic call from my sister-in-law. Apparently one of her cats had a urinary infection. My wife got all the details, but this family cat crisis clearly illustrates how today's affluent have changed.

My sister-in-law owns a small condominium in midtown Manhattan, and it costs her a small fortune. She is also the doting owner of five cats. Our family has enjoyed her company in what used to be three to four visits a year: long weekends, Christmas and Fourths of July at the beach, etc. These visits have now dwindled to one—over Christmas, and not even the entire week. When I asked about the reason, my sister-in-law claimed she was "going broke" boarding her cats. She was spending more on boarding charges than she was on airfare!

The day following the feline emergency, she called back to give my wife an update. The crisis was over: little kitty was medicated and on the mend, and her emergency vet bill was $2,000!

This is driving a demand not just for skilled general-practice veterinarians and medical specialists, but for anyone who can provide dog-walking, cat-sitting and pet psychotherapy for the "Mittens" and "Rovers" in affluent households. Some pet-related services may seem bizarre, but as long as the affluent are willing to pay, the demand will be met. Recently, one California start-up made a splash by "renting dogs" to people who enjoy canine companionship, but don't want the hassles associated with actually caring for these critters.

> Marlena Cervantes, founder of FlexPetz, bristles when people refer to her five-month-old business as a rent-a-pet service. She prefers the term "shared pet ownership," explaining the concept is more akin to a vacation time share or a gym membership than a trip to the video store.
>
> "Our members are responsible in that they realize full-time ownership is not an option for them and would be unfair to the dog," said Cervantes, 32, a behavioral therapist who got the idea while working with pets and autistic children. "It prevents dogs from being adopted and then returned to the shelter by people who realize it wasn't a good fit."
>
> FlexPetz is currently available in Los Angeles and San Diego, where Cervantes lives. She plans to open new locations in San Francisco next month, and in New York in September and London by the end of the year.
>
> She's also hoping to franchise the FlexPetz concept so the dogs will have housing options other than kennels when not in use. For San Francisco, she has hired a caretaker who plans to keep the dogs at her house when they are not on loan to members.
>
> For an annual fee of $99.95, a monthly payment of $49.95 and a per-visit charge of $39.95 a day (discounted to $24.95 Sunday through Thursday), animal lovers who enroll in FlexPetz get to spend time with a four-legged companion from

> Cervantes' 10-dog crew of Afghan hounds, Labrador retrievers and Boston terriers.
>
> The membership costs cover the expense of training the dogs, boarding them at a cage-free kennel, home or office delivery, collar-sized global positioning devices, veterinary bills and liability insurance. It also pays for the "care kits"; comprised of leashes, bowls, beds and pre-measured food; that accompany each dog on its visits.

Is renting dogs a silly idea? Only time will tell. It's certainly no sillier than marketing "pet rocks" to young baby boomers or selling "cage free eggs" to affluent households willing to pay three times more for a carton to ensure (in theory) that a bunch of chickens they will never see are treated humanely. All of this takes on a weird flavor when approached in isolation, but when blended in to every other aspect of today's affluent, it seems more acceptable. For that matter, is any of this more ridiculous than an affluent family selling a 4,000-square-foot home in which they raised three children and, as empty nesters, upgrading to an 8,500-square-foot home in a gated community?

The affluent family, though far more fractured and complex than it used to be, is one of the most influential factors in today's top quintile decision making. Whether it's new cars for newly licensed children drivers, exotic vacations, pet extravagance, second homes, dream homes or luxury retirement communities, the affluent family, in all of its dimensions, is an extremely lucrative market.

In the next chapter, you'll discover how interwoven family health and financial health have really become.

Research Facts

- A large majority—92%—of children whose families make more than $75,000 a year—live with two parents (including stepparents).
- 87 percent of grandparents buy clothing for their grandkids; 80 percent buy books; 76 percent purchase toys; and 45 percent give their grandkids videos and DVDs.
- For the first time since the Depression, more Americans ages 75 and older have been leaving the South than moving there.
- Some of the "hot retirement spots" named by The Wall Street Journal and MSNBC include: Ashland, Oregon; San Antonio, Texas; New Bern and Mount Airy, North Carolina; and St. George, Utah.
- Upscale assisted-living is a booming industry.
- Almost $17 billion a year is spent directly marketing to children, even for adult goods like cars.

6

Financial Health

Among the working affluent, 82% give high or medium priority to meeting current living expenses.

—2007 "Understanding the Affluent" research study

The connection that the affluent make between their *personal* and *family* key motivators and their *financial health* is real and readily visible. In fact, all of the key motivators are inextricably linked. The top quintile has more resources than 80% of the population, so it's unsurprising to discover that there's a direct correlation between personal motivators and how/where the affluent spend their hard-earned money.

It's not as though money is everything to maturing boomers, but it *is* directly responsible for their lifestyles, spending patterns, and in many instances, their stress levels. Social psychologists often refer to this as the "affluent paradox," since money impacts virtually everything about them—who they are, where they live, how much they work and what they do for fun.

When it comes to financial health, affluent boomers consider topics like the following:

- "Cash flow is tight, but I need to maintain our lifestyle."
- "I wonder if I'm getting the unbiased financial advice I need."
- "There's got to be some way to get more deductions."
- "I hope we can maintain our lifestyle when I retire."
- "I need to get someone to review my financial plan."

- "I hate all this financial paperwork. I don't even know where our important papers are."
- "I hope we have enough in the kids' educational account to fund graduate school."

Regardless of the skepticism and distrust that top-quintile Americans display toward sellers of products and services, and the financial services industry in particular, financial services professionals should know that they're in the right profession at the right time. Whether you're a financial advisor or planner, broker, banker, accountant or trusts and estates lawyer, you are probably already targeting the affluent market.

For example, an Oechsli Institute 2005 research study (*Attracting New Affluent Clients*) revealed that 95% of financial advisors target prospects with at least $250,000 in investable assets. Of the 819 financial advisors responding to our survey, most were very clear about the asset level they target, and the minimum level they'll accept from a new client. Their efforts to capture affluent clients are written into business plans and incorporated into training programs. For some professionals, becoming a "rainmaker" is akin to finding the Holy Grail.

Yet that same study showed that only 7% of financial advisors who target clients with $1 million or more in investable assets are able to grab the "brass ring"—to secure at least 10 new affluent accounts each year. While it would be foolish to extrapolate these figures to members of related professions, it's a good bet that most people offering financial products and services to the top quintile do *not* acquire 10 or more affluent clients each year. The reasons are clear. The average financial services professional doesn't truly understand the financial motivations of the affluent prospect.

An Unbiased Go-To Pro

To begin with, the affluent are looking for an *unbiased* financial professional—someone they trust to put their interests first and guide them through the complexities of today's financial world. They want the financial equivalent of a family doctor.

Mature boomers are well aware that their financial health is multifaceted and impacts every aspect of their life. Most already have an accountant, but recognize that they need someone who can do more than compile yearly tax returns. Most have invested money in the stock market, but recognize that they need more than someone advising them in their stock and bond purchases. Most own insurance policies, but recognize that they need someone who does more than sell insurance. They want a professional—someone unbiased—someone to oversee the entirety of their family's financial affairs: in effect, someone to look after their *financial health.*

By "unbiased professional," I'm referring to the individual who is not perceived as a salesperson. This professional must place the client's interests above her own, even if her decisions result in less revenue for herself and her firm. Our research projects point to a high level of distrust of financial professionals. Much of this is due to the old days of transaction fees. Stockbrokers used to make money by changing clients' positions in different securities, which was not always in the clients' best interests.

Today, most financial advisors are moving to a different fee structure. They receive a certain percentage of each client's invested assets each year (around 1%), which creates a more unbiased approach. When the client does well, the advisor does well. Everybody's equally happy (or unhappy). However, many financial professionals are learning that this fee for "unbiased advice" must be earned. They are also discovering that "unbiased advice" is not a good marketing slogan, since it insinuates that the inverse also exists: biased advice. And as Judy's financial advisor learned, poor service plants the seeds of dissatisfaction, which leads to losing your affluent clients.

This concept also applies to providers of goods and services outside the realm of financial services. In every aspect of life, the top quintile feels it is being manipulated. Wealthy Americans want service providers who provide unfiltered communication and have their best interests in mind.

From the perspective of the affluent, however, becoming a go-to financial professional is easier said than done. In their minds, every institution and individual connected to finance is making similar promises. Everyone claims to be a "go-to" financial expert or wealth manager. Everyone claims to provide all the needed services. On top of all that, when you factor in the walking-talking contradiction that many boomers have become, one Latin phrase known to every affluent prospect is "caveat emptor." Obviously, this creates a real challenge.

Our 1999 Research study on the affluent, *Capturing the Affluent Investor,* revealed significant gaps between advisor performance and investor expectations. With a 95.2% validation factor, survey respondents reported that their financial professionals were not meeting their expectations in 14 of the 20 qualities associated with sound financial professional standards. Our research in June of 2004, leading to the Research Report *Determining How the Affluent Make Major Purchase Decisions,* not only validated these performance gaps, but revealed that they had grown more significant. Our latest study, reflected in Chart 6-1, offers yet another sobering glimpse into the trust issue.

Chart 6-1

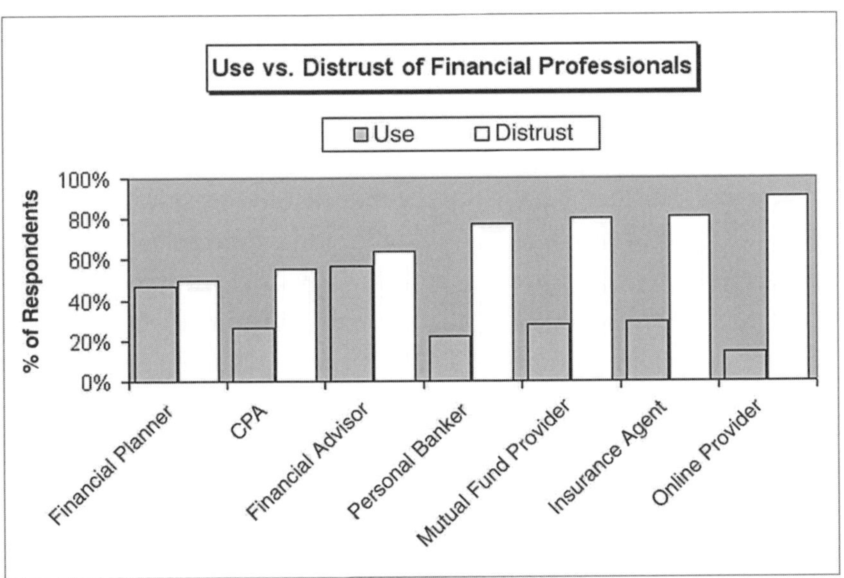

Many affluent investors use several different investment sources (two or more financial advisors, insurance agents, financial planners, company retirement plans, etc.). The go-to financial advisor tries to directly manage as much of his client's assets as possible. He works to understand a client's complete financial picture (even assets outside of his management) to ensure that all components work together. He wants to be consulted for all financial decisions.

For instance, when we asked the affluent what's important to them, they told us they want a Primary Financial Coordinator that:

- Is proactive about contacting clients when upcoming tax and other changes will impact their investment portfolio.
- Clearly reveals his fee structure.
- Clearly understands the client's goals and family situation when giving investment advice.
- Brings in experts to help with other financial areas.
- Helps clients select the best asset mix for their investment portfolios.
- Helps clients create formal financial plans.
- Helps clients coordinate and organize all of their financial documents.
- Coordinates investment decisions.

"A Bad Rap"

Thanks to the historical nature of the industry and negative press associated with recent research analysis and mutual fund share class cases, the financial services industry is still viewed as an instrument through which to buy and sell stocks. Most affluent individuals DO perceive a need for an insurance provider, a CPA, an estate planning attorney and a stockbroker, but our research indicates that they don't fully understand that a financial advisor can bring all these services to the table and act as a coordinator for those services.

Also, because everyone associated with the financial world is making similar claims, the consumer is confused. Unless a financial salesperson is exceptional, and works hard to reposition his services, he's likely to be perceived in the manner in which the relationship began—i.e., as a stockbroker, insurance agent, CPA, etc.

Despite this, any firm that develops the necessary wealth management platforms, effectively trains its distribution force, avoids negative headlines (especially regarding fraudulent sales practices), and keeps its distribution force current on the best ways to deal with affluent idiosyncrasies, will be well positioned to capitalize on affluent opportunities. By wealth management platforms, I refer to:

1) Budgeting, cash-flow management and determining net worth.
2) Banking services.
3) Insurance planning.
4) Investment administration (asset management).
5) Education planning.
6) Tax planning.
7) Retirement planning.
8) Estate Planning.
9) Charitable giving.

Training must encompass both wealth management services and platforms. There needs to be a strong working knowledge of the services and solutions provided, and there is a profound need for high-level training in the "art of selling to the affluent." Because the affluent don't like salespeople, any professional attempting to market and sell products or services, especially financial services, must refine her sales skills to the point where they appear seamless. In other words: invisible. That's not an easy task.

Buyer Beware

Headlines such as this one by AP reporter Marcy Gordon—*Probe of "Free Lunch" Seminars Finds Sales Pressure, Misleading Claims, Fraud* (September 10, 2007, Yahoo! Finance)—don't help. They elevate the level of distrust that aging boomers already have toward the financial services industry. The net result is more skepticism and confusion.

Regardless of how much money is invested in advertising, trusted advisors and the solutions available, word-of-mouth influence and the prospect's personal experiences will prevail. For every financial advisor who uses a branding campaign to get in the door but fails to embody that brand, negative word-of-mouth influence is unleashed. And those negative headlines are then recalled to validate their adverse "gut" impression.

Wealth management platforms without effective training are not the answer. Likewise, training without proper wealth management tools will not meet the demands of the affluent. *Both* are required. But for training to be effective, it must include sales training. As the following chart illustrates, the sales techniques used by most financial professionals are no longer effective.

A silver lining becomes visible when you consider that 80.3% of the affluent have an interest in a financial coordinator. This means they have a high level of dissatisfaction with their *current* financial professionals and would be open to a change. This presents a tremendous opportunity for professionals who take time to fully understand the affluent, provide the services they need, and accomplish this with a high degree of professionalism and personalized service.

Chart 6-2

Financial Advisors Prospecting Methods: Use and Results

Prospecting Method	Percentage who USED this Method	Percentage who Brought in NEW CLIENTS using this Method
Direct Mail	57%	27%
Cold Calling	46%	27%
Seminars	62%	40%
Networking*	93%	78%
Asking for Referrals*	97%	90%
Asking for Introductions*	91%	72%

*High-impact Activities

As state regulators and the Securities and Exchange Commission re-examine marketing practices as they relate to "free lunch" seminars for seniors, aging boomers will require a higher degree of trust before allowing someone to advise them on their financial affairs. The affluent will insist upon more personal interaction, but will also make it increasingly more challenging to engage in this type of contact.

Again, we've run smack-dab into their contradictory nature. Financial health is one of their top motivators: they want a trusted professional to advise them on the multi-dimensional aspects of their financial affairs, billions of dollars are being thrown at them marketing the solution, and their trust level is at an all-time low. Chart 6-3 is an indication of the heavy lifting required by financial professionals attempting to work with this high-maintenance, dichotomous species.

The affluent understand that credentials are often misleading. CFP, CFA, CIMA, CFS, ChFC, CLU, CPA, CPA/PFS . . . represent just a portion of the alphabet soup of credentials printed on the business cards

Chart 6-3

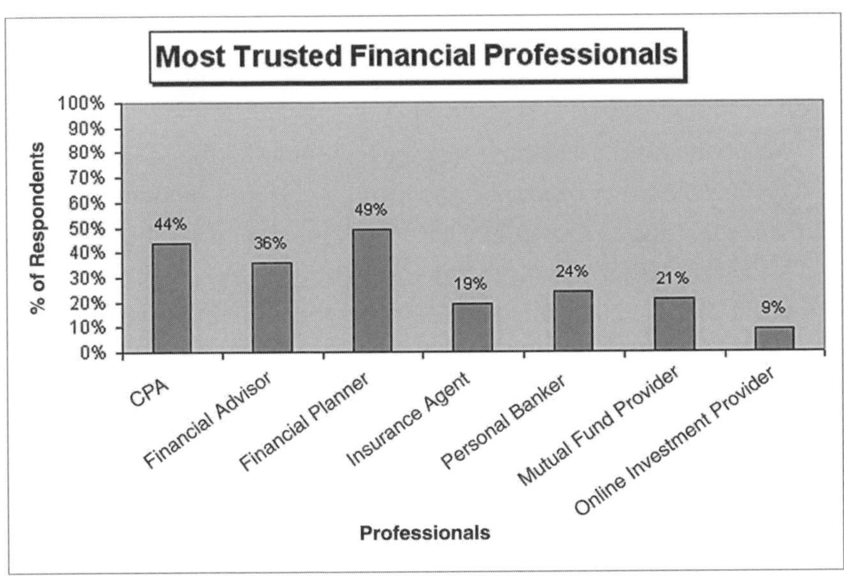

of financial professionals. And confusion about credentials seems to have contributed to the general distrust of financial professionals.

Amid this alphabet soup, other than the CPA, the *Certified Financial Planner* designation holds the most significance with the affluent. This is not to suggest that the CFP designation is superior to the others, but that it more accurately reflects the current needs and wants of the affluent.

The affluent want a true financial plan. The research is quite clear on the importance the wealthy place on having a financial plan that is current, comprehensive, and created by a professional with expertise in financial planning. From their perspective, who could be better equipped to provide this service than a *Certified Financial Planner*? Naturally, this doesn't mean that everyone must become a *Certified Financial Planner.* But it does mean that financial professionals working with the affluent should have access to a designated CFP to provide planning services.

The top quintile doesn't make much distinction between *financial advisor* and *financial planner* when it comes to retirement planning. Within the world of financial services, there is ongoing debate about the legal distinctions between *financial advisor* and *financial planner*, but they have become blurred in the eyes of the affluent. It is important to note that this obfuscation most often occurs among *financial advisors* and *financial planners* who are addressing affluent needs accordingly.

What we found interesting was the low standing the affluent give a *CPA, personal banker, insurance agent,* and *online provider* regarding retirement planning as shown in Chart 6-4. This should not be perceived as a knock on CPAs: as you just discovered, they are among the most trusted of all financial professionals. What the affluent are telling us is that they want CPAs to stick to their knitting. The same holds true for bankers, insurance agents, and online providers. Once again, this presents a tremendous opportunity for any financial professional, especially *financial advisors* and *financial planners*, who possess expertise in the retirement market.

The dominant focus of the affluent is on lifestyle. After lifestyle

Chart 6-4

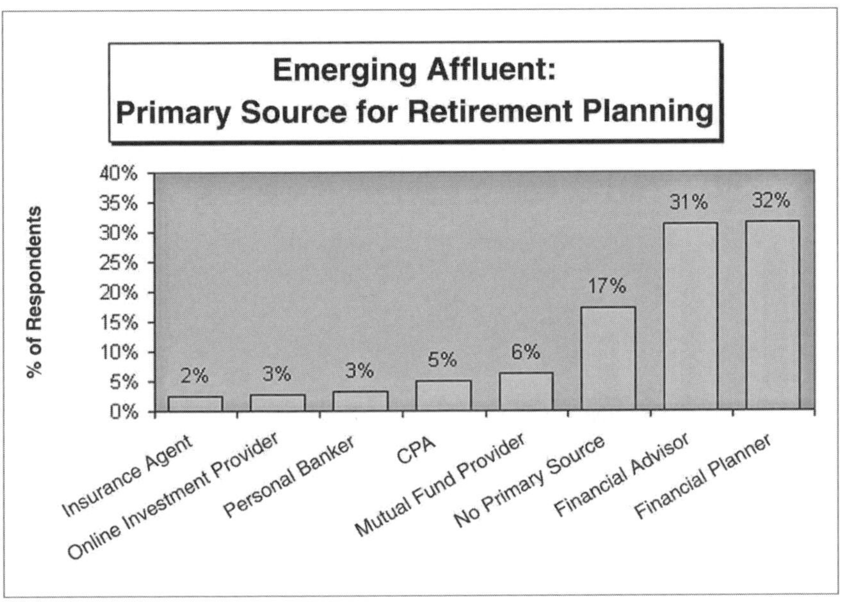

concerns, affluent boomers consider keeping *financial documents organized* and *minimizing taxes* as their most important financial priorities. The affluent are making a connection between keeping *financial documents organized* and *minimizing taxes* to the importance they place on lifestyle issues—current and future.

These findings reflect the lack of confidence in their past or existing relationship(s) with individual financial professionals, as well as that major institutions (government and corporate America) will offer much assistance in these areas. Financial professionals need to be doing more than just focusing on investments: they need to focus on the nuts and bolts of their clients' day-to-day lives.

Working Affluent versus Retired Affluent

Working affluent boomers, those still in their peak earning years, are very concerned with minimizing taxes, as shown in Chart 6-5. It's in-

Chart 6-5

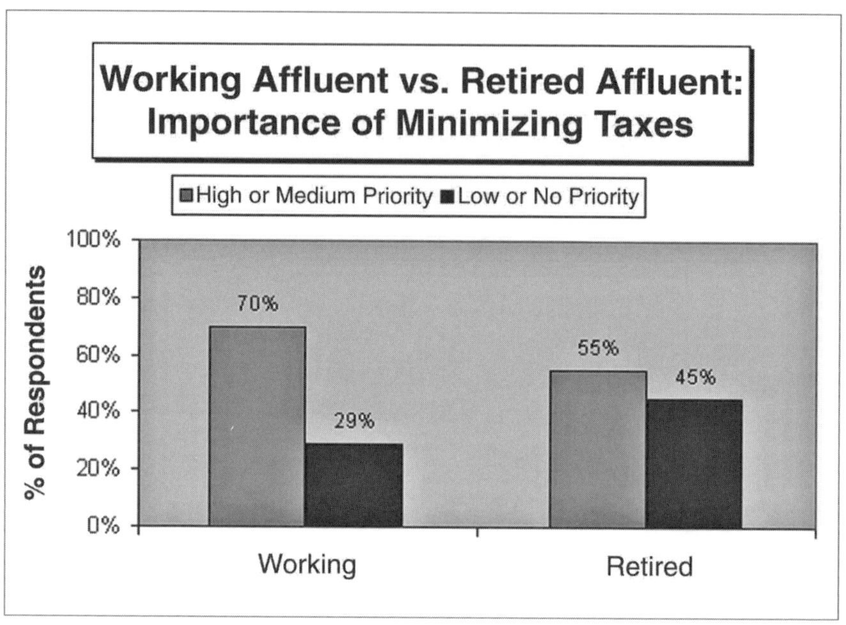

teresting to note, however, that more than half of the retired affluent still express concern with the amount of taxes they pay.

Reducing debt is a low priority for the majority of the retired affluent. Maintaining their current lifestyles requires a certain amount of debt. Prime-aged boomers are accustomed to debt as they lease, rather than own, their automobiles, and they simply factor it into their cost of living. Although many of the wealthy may be concerned about outliving their resources, most retired affluent have reduced their debt to minimal levels. This makes debt reduction statistically insignificant among the retired affluent.

Affluent Men versus Affluent Women

Affluent women put significantly more emphasis on financial planning than affluent men. This does not mean that affluent men are not interested in financial planning. They are. But affluent women place a higher degree of trust in a *financial planner* than they place in a *finan-*

Chart 6-6

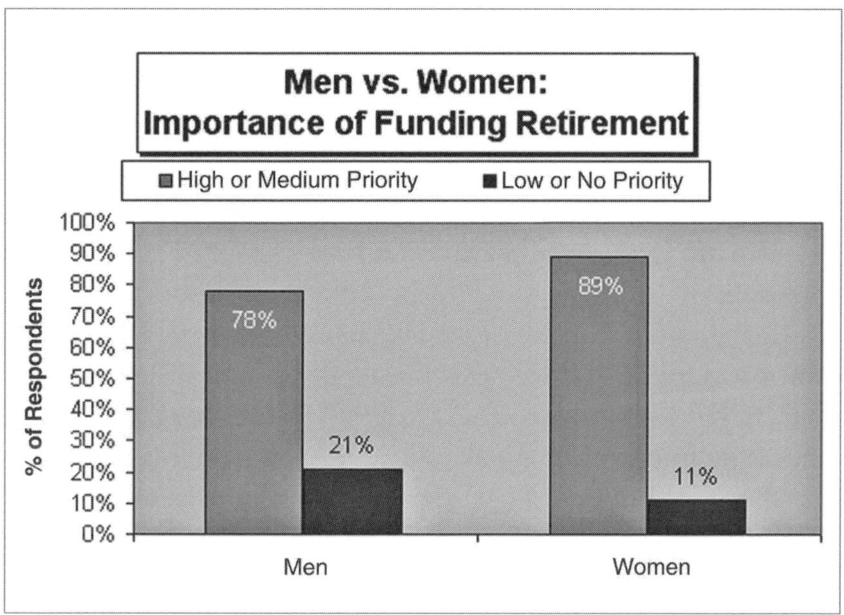

cial advisor, because they are more likely to want (and then act on) the plan that's created. Affluent men tend to procrastinate.

Affluent women are playing an increasingly significant role in their families' major purchases, with lifestyle issues a major concern. It's important for any financial professional to recognize the role of women regarding family finances and ensure they earn the trust of the woman of the household.

Both affluent men and affluent women place a high priority on funding their retirement, as shown in Chart 6-6. However, retirement planning is much more important to women. In addition, affluent women place greater emphasis on funding current living expenses, debt reduction, tax minimization, financial protection, property protection, financial consolidation and financial organization than affluent men.

Financial professionals interested in becoming "go-to" financial coordinators must develop a healthy working relationship with the woman of the household, and be able to competently handle the concerns listed above.

Top-quintile females are less likely than males to use the Internet for assistance with financial decisions. But that doesn't diminish the growing role that online sources play in the lives of both men and women. For the wealthy, the Internet is becoming ever-more important for conducting pre-purchase research and obtaining post-sale service. Therefore, financial professionals must have more than just an online "presence."

Neither affluent men nor women are responsive to cold calls, as shown in Chart 6-7. They detest them! Hence, this marketing technique is *very* ineffective—often counterproductive—and the financial services industry would be *well* advised to avoid this activity. Because the affluent do not like salespeople, cold-calling often reinforces negative stereotypes of both salespeople and the financial services industry.

Neither affluent men nor women are overly concerned with reducing debt, which is consistent with the importance they place on lifestyle issues. Interestingly, affluent men are more concerned that a financial professional understand their personal goals than affluent women, as

Chart 6-7

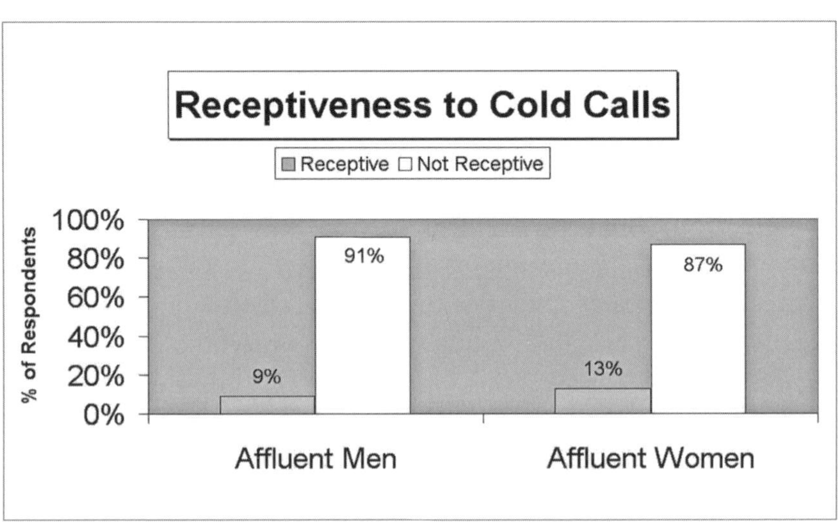

referenced in Chart 6-8. On the surface, this appears to be a contradiction, considering the importance women place on planning and funding retirement. But the issue here is about *understanding* the goals versus the actual planning or funding of retirement. Affluent men *do* have goals and they want those advising them on *financial health* to make time to fully understand the goals.

Women also have goals and, likewise, want a professional to understand those goals, but they're more likely to concentrate on the necessary planning and funding.

Over two-thirds of affluent respondents placed a significant degree of importance on getting all of their financial affairs organized. This speaks to a number of issues in the financial world. Increasing complexity has reached the point where the affluent no longer consider it desirable to make isolated financial decisions. Also, because the volume of paperwork required by financial institutions is overwhelming, the affluent want someone to help them sort through what's important and what's not.

Opportunity awaits any financial institution or professional who consistently delivers the brand *as promised.* But financial institutions

Chart 6-8

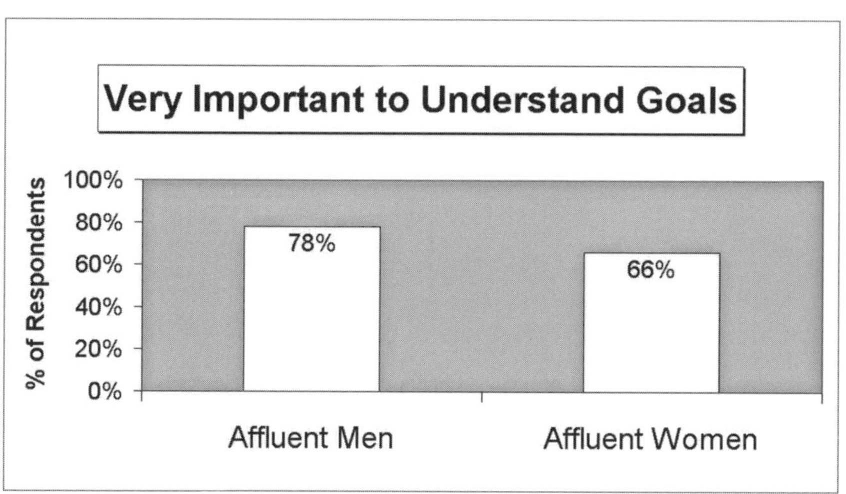

must work hard at quality control regarding the training, marketing and sales tactics of their distribution force. Any sales corps is only as strong as its weakest link. Therefore, it takes only a few bad apples to spoil the barrel.

Research Facts

- The affluent are looking for an *unbiased* financial professional—someone they trust to put their interests first and guide them through the complexities of today's financial world. They want the financial equivalent of a family doctor.
- Our 1999 study, *Capturing the Affluent Investor*, revealed significant gaps between advisor performance and investor expectations.
- 80.3% of the affluent have an interest in a financial coordinator, which means they have a high level of dissatisfaction with their current financial professionals, and would be open to a change.
- Aside from lifestyle concerns, the affluent believe that organizing financial documents and minimizing taxes are the most important financial priorities.

7

Spiritual Health

Charitable giving is a low priority for America's affluent.
—2007 "Understanding the Affluent" research study

Now that the initial wave of affluent boomers is in their 60s, gerontologists are not predicting a happy group of post-retirees. On the contrary, they envision that large numbers will be totally unprepared. "We are going to have a whole generation of people who are wealthy, healthy, and bored," said Dr. Dorothy Cantor, co-author of *What Do You Want to DO When You Grow Up?* and a former president of the American Psychological Association.[32]

Some might question how healthy they will be, but one thing is certain: they will be the healthiest and most populous generation of their age group in history. So herein is the connection to *spiritual health.* It's almost as though the aging affluent boomers are already gearing up to belie Dr. Cantor's dire forecast.

As the following charts indicate, maturing affluent boomers currently in the workforce are concerned about meeting current living expenses, but also consider themselves quite spiritual. This is why Dr. Cantor's prediction about bored hordes of retiring wealthy may not come to pass. Our research is quite clear: affluent boomers' focus on

[32] Claudia H. Deutsch, "Never Too Early; Training to be Old." *The New York Times,* April 10, 2007.

financing their lifestyle often creates stress, and that stress influences their decisions regarding *spiritual health.*

Chart 7-1	
Aging and Beyond	
Percentage of people 50 and over who agree with these statements:	
I am a spiritual person.	87%
I am a religious person.	82%
My confidence in life after death has increased with age.	66%
Thinking about my own death scares me.	20%

Source AARP
USA Today, September 25, 2007, USA TODAY Snapshots, front page

"Spirituality" is an ephemeral term—a will-o'-the-wisp that eludes our grasp unless we translate spiritual concepts into the concrete and the material. Unless spirituality is made manifest as sets of values, behavior patterns and—for the purposes of this book—spending patterns that can be tracked, categorized and analyzed, it's impossible to determine how "unearthly" matters actually matter to the affluent and, therefore, how they affect the American economy. Unless there are still people paying for indulgences—"Get-Out-of-Hell" cards sold by the medieval church—we cannot measure the importance that spirituality has for *anyone.*

Therefore, we must let God reign in Heaven and let the Universe keep the galaxies spinning, and focus instead on how affluent Americans spend their money on planet Earth—on such relatively mundane things as charitable giving, travel and self-help books, as well as efforts to protect the environment for future generations. Some of what we've discovered may surprise you.

Percentage who rate Religion as very to extremely important:

Affluent—57% Non-affluent—67%

2005 Gallup Polls

Not the Most Giving of People

Despite the well-publicized philanthropy of people like Bill and Melinda Gates, Warren Buffet and a cornucopia of Hollywood celebrities, affluent Americans are not the most giving of people, regardless of how they perceive themselves. Fact is: charitable giving ranks low on the list of priorities for the top quintile—mostly because their focus is internal. It's all about them. Serve them, cater to their needs, wants and desires, and you will score well. Fail them, and you may score lower than the Department of Motor Vehicles (depicted on the television comedy *Reaper* as a portal to Hell). This isn't to say the affluent don't donate—and donate generously—to charities. But their donations are less than you might imagine, and they're often tinged with self interest. Even the super-rich are relatively stingy:

> . . . the move by Mr. Buffet raises the question of exactly what the other billionaires do have in mind for their money. According to the economist Christopher Carroll at Johns Hopkins University, in his article, "Why Do the Rich Save so Much?," the seemingly obvious question of why people would want so much money turns out to be a real puzzle.
>
> The rational economic argument for accumulating wealth says that people want to use it for something: to spend, to give it to their families to enhance their future standard of living or to do something philanthropic.
>
> When you look at the Slate 60 list, however, you see that philanthropy can't be the main reason. For all of their amazing generosity, the super-rich typically do not give away their entire fortunes, or even a big share. That's what makes Mr. Buffet so notable.
>
> For 2006, the Slate 60, not including Mr. Buffett, pledged or gave a little over $7 billion to charity. Yet as of September 2006, the 60 richest Americans had an estimated $630 billion of wealth, up more than $62 billion (about 10 percent) from the

year before. People are accumulating money much faster than they are giving it away.[33]

And these are the super-rich!

Gifting is important to the affluent, but most donate less than $10,000 in their wills to charity. And most give to charities representing causes that have personally affected them—to organizations fighting Alzheimer's disease after a parent becomes afflicted with the condition, to AIDS research if a friend contracts the disease, and to breast cancer research if a spouse or friend is afflicted.

Yes, the affluent do tithe and donate to their places of worship—whether they're Christian, Jewish, Muslim, Buddhist or Hindu—but they are more likely to give money to their *local* churches, synagogues or temples rather than larger religious organizations or foundations.

The chart below illustrates how the importance of various financial areas does not change very much once affluent boomers retire, with charitable giving remaining at the bottom of what's considered highly important.

Chart 7-2

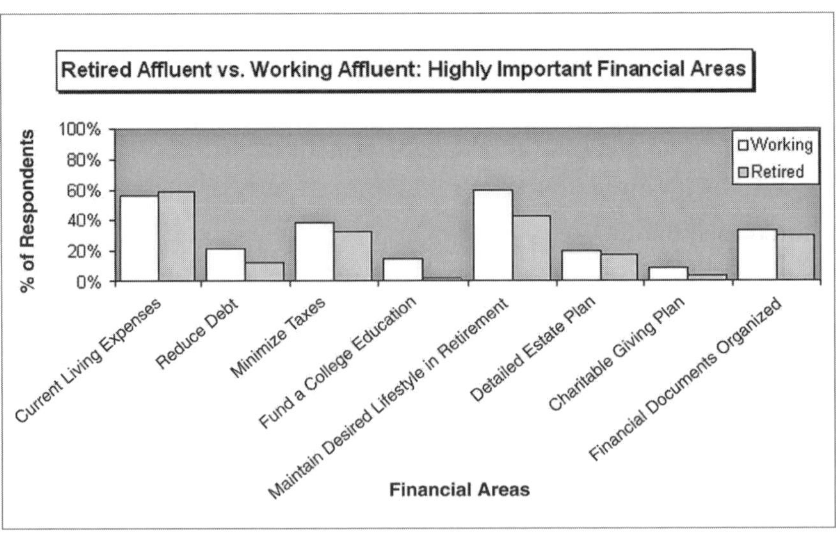

[33] Austan Goolsbee, "Why Do the Richest People Rarely Intend to Give it All Away?" *The New York Times*, March 1, 2007.

This isn't to say that affluent boomers are so self-absorbed that they're unwilling to help others. Instead, it reflects their distrust of institutionalized charitable organizations. Remember, affluent boomers are a highly suspicious lot. And as you already know, aging affluent boomers have been cash-flowing a luxurious lifestyle, often leaving little or no money to spare.

Because human being are infinitely capable of rationalizing, I tell most of my financial services clients that they shouldn't waste time trying to convince people to donate to charity. Affluent attitudes toward charity may be strong, but when it comes to actually pulling out the checkbook, don't hold your breath.

In part, this is because many of the affluent have confronted situations like that of "Paul," who once worked for a major metropolitan newspaper. During his first year as a copyboy, Paul was approached by a colleague soliciting money for a large, well-known charitable foundation. When he offered to donate a certain sum—representing about 25% of his weekly paycheck—it was *strongly* implied that if he hoped to "move up the ladder," he would "give 'til it hurt." Understandably, he considered this extortion, and was especially infuriated when he later learned (with the rest of the country) that more than 90% of his donations were going to "administrative expenses"—i.e., he was paying bureaucrats' salaries instead of helping needy people.

For this reason, and others, the affluent are wary of donating hard-earned dollars to large philanthropic organizations. And for this reason, and others, they prefer to toss $100 onto the collection plate at church each Sunday, because they know where the money is going. (A lot of this has to do with personal control: remember, most of the affluent are entrepreneurs, business managers and top salespeople.)

The New Age?

As educated and thoughtful people, the affluent are driving sales of self-help, religious and "New Age" books in an effort to achieve enlightenment. For the publishing industry, spirituality is big business. *Publisher's Weekly* determined that of the 10,000 consumers it surveyed in

2004, 18% had purchased at least one spiritual or religious book during the previous year, accounting for nearly 7% of the book industry's $28.6 billion in revenues that year.[34]

Beyond books such as the Bible, *The Purpose Driven Life* and the *Tao Te Ching*, many affluent Americans seek solace and spend money on experiential luxuries. For these consumers, luxury is not to be found in a brand name or material product, but in experiences—whether the experiences constitute weeks of adventure travel, a day of pampering at the local spa or few hours at a restaurant specializing in the world's premier beluga caviar and champagne. It's not about products; it's not about services; it's about thoroughly *experiencing* these products and services.

> . . . [A]s in their 20s, aging baby boomers have taken up the quest for meaning, as their three-decade infatuation with accumulating "stuff" wanes in the face of mortality, or just the realization that there's not that much more left to buy. If they no longer seek to transform the world by revolution, they strive at least to improve a small part of it, or perhaps themselves, through adventure, experience and self-actualization.
>
> . . . [T]he leading edge of the boomer generation, now in the shadow of 60, [is looking] at some of the ways in which they pursue transcendence through leisure. Some are taking volunteer-service trips to aid the impoverished inhabitants of the more colorful and exotic parts of the world. Others are exploring organic, gourmet, locally sourced cuisine that minimizes the carbon footprint of their dinners. They are settling in "spa lifestyle" developments combining the twin obsessions of aging boomers: real estate and aerobic conditioning. And they are boarding flights for "heritage tours" that connect them to ancestors whose foresight in migrating to America was richly vindicated by the eventual birth of baby boomers themselves.[35]

[34] Dennis Coday, "Doctrines Are Benchmarks of Wisdom: Among Confusion of Spiritual Resources, Tradition Offers Guides." National Catholic Reporter, July 15, 2005.
[35] Jerry Adler, "Meaningful Pursuits." *Newsweek*, August 6, 2007.

Selfless and selfish; spiritual and self-congratulatory: this pretty much defines the boomers—at least the oldest and most affluent members.

The Value of Experiences

I'm not suggesting that taking adventure cruises to Antarctica to pet penguins or sipping Bordeaux in Bordeaux is going to land anyone reserved parking in Heaven, but what's important to remember is that affluent boomers and Gen-Xers are more concerned with the value of the experiential than their forebears. In some ways, of course, there's nothing new under the sun. Many of "robber barons" of the Gilded Age crossed the Atlantic on luxury liners to reach vacation homes in France and England. The difference today, however, is that 19th century tycoons *had* to travel by steamship, whereas today's affluent Americans *choose* to take "slow boats" in order to *experience* the luxury of fine dining, Monte Carlo-style casinos and luxury cabins that only the world's premier cruise lines can offer.

One reason for the increased focus on experience may be due to the fact that, despite remarkable productivity gains made throughout the 20th and early 21st centuries, leisure time has not really increased.

> . . . 70 percent of the decline in hours worked has been offset by an increase in hours spent in school. [And] contrary to conventional wisdom, average hours spent in home production are actually slightly higher now than in the early part of the 20th Century. Finally, leisure time per capita is approximately the same as it was in 1900.[36]

Of course, measuring leisure time is nearly as difficult as measuring wealth through the ages. By today's standards, Julius Caesar would be considered a multi-billionaire. Of course, Caesar didn't have what many of us consider necessities today—from air conditioning and refrigerators to television sets and DVD players—"stuff" that even the

---

36 Ramey, Valerie A. and Francis, Neville. "A Century of Work and Leisure," abstract, May 2006.

least affluent now take for granted. But Caesar and his heirs did enjoy the luxury of at least *some* leisure time—a concept completely alien to the average working man until the 20th century.

It's no surprise then, that when baby boomers aren't helping Third-World villagers digs wells for potable water, they're enjoying products and services once reserved for the super-rich. They are experiencing things that only dukes and lords enjoyed a hundred years ago. They know that the only things they can "take with them" are not material possessions, but what's imprinted in their memories. It may sound corny, but savvy marketers know that there's plenty of dough in that there corn.

When it comes to matters of the spirit, our research has determined that the affluent often think in these terms:

- "I need to start going back to church / temple."
- "I need to get more in touch with my spiritual side."
- "I need to give more to my church / temple." Yes they're thinking that, but your job it to transform thoughts into actions.
- "When the time comes, how do I distribute my estate?" (Financial services professional take note!)
- "Pop's lived a good life. I know I'll see him in heaven. (Funeral services and related professionals take note!)
- I want give something back, and spend more time helping others.
- I'm thinking of a complete career change.

In sum, any product or service provider who offers the affluent an opportunity to experience, thrills, chills, excitement and spiritual enlightenment is well positioned to sell to this growing market. Where previous generations of the wealthy were concerned about the status that particular products conferred, today's boomer affluent (with few exceptions) could care less about proving their status. For one thing (as noted), most affluent Americans don't believe that they're particularly rich. At the same time, they want to enjoy the fruits of their 50+ hour work weeks by fishing for marlin on the weekends, or jetting to Key West to "slum" with a crew of Ernest Hemingway look-alikes at the original "Sloppy Joes."

Take note.

Research Facts

- In general, the affluent are suspicious of large charitable organizations, preferring to give to local faith-based groups or charities representing causes that have personally affected them.
- The typical affluent American donates about $10,000 in his will to charity.
- The boomer generation has tired of accumulating "stuff," and now prefers to accumulate experiences.
- Many affluent baby boomers are not prepared mentally, physically or financially for their glory years—retirement.
- 87% of those over 50 consider themselves a "spiritual person."

SECTION III

Marketing to the Affluent

8

Do's and Don'ts

The enlightened sales professional looks for opportunities to associate his product or service with career achievements of the prospect.

—*Selling to the Affluent* by Thomas J. Stanley

Thanks to my hectic travel schedule, I didn't bother purchasing a desktop computer for a number of years. I used a laptop for word-processing and general computing. But as any true "road warrior" will attest, laptops take a beating in "the field." And, since this piece of equipment must take a licking but keep on ticking, warranties and dependability are crucial. Because the service and quality of Dell and Gateway were experiencing hic-cups, I recently purchased a new laptop from a local, owner-operated computer store recommended by an associate. My friend also suggested that I purchase the latest "workhorse"—a fully loaded IBM, even though it was more costly. After purchasing the machine, along with a three-year warranty and upgrade package, I'd spent nearly $1,000 more that I intended. But heck, you get what you pay for, right?

Well . . . not always.

Don't Hassle the Affluent!

Within a week, I noticed that my laptop was slow to boot up. So, I returned to the store and left my computer for a diagnosis. When I returned to pick it up, I was told that everything appeared to be working properly. Hmm.

Two weeks later, I returned with the same problem, but after a few days, I was told that—once again—everything checked out. This time, however, I was presented with a bill for $45. When I questioned the bill, I was informed that the warranty I purchased was through IBM, and even though the store owner sold me this machine, he was not responsible for any problems—i.e., I had to pay for his services.

I contacted the IBM Warranty Claims department, filing a complaint about both my computer and this retailer. To make a long story short, IBM fixed my laptop and forwarded a written apology for the retailer's behavior and any misunderstandings and inconveniences to which I'd been subjected. (In the meantime, negative word-of-mouth began mysteriously spreading about this local retailer.)

Presently, another laptop component—my power cord—malfunctioned, so I called an IBM claims representative only to discover that IBM had sold its PC division to a Chinese company called Lenovo. I proceeded to discuss the problem, filled out more paperwork, received a case number, and once again shipped my computer to IBM (Lenovo) for repairs.

The following week, IBM (Lenovo) informed me that my laptop's warranty had expired, and asked permission to charge $650 to fix the machine. Bewildered, I read my warranty form aloud, and the gentleman on the other end of the line asked that I fax this information so he could "look into it." When this gentleman called a week later, he told me that the individual who serviced my warranty claim and wrote the letter was no longer employed by IBM (Lenovo), that the serial numbers of the machine didn't match, and I needed to pay $650.

How would you have responded?

I asked to speak with a supervisor (who happened to be on vacation that day, so I left her a voice mail). Three working days later, I had a similar discussion with this supervisor, after calling her a second time. To date, I still don't have my laptop, and I've since purchased a non-IBM replacement.

I've also told this story to anyone who will listen.

Lessons from the Don'ts

IBM (Lenovo) is not alone in its struggles to please affluent customers. Our research is very clear that solving problems quickly and satisfactorily is critical when it comes to earning the loyalty of your affluent clientele. The research also states that the *quality* of a warranty is statistically significant when making an initial purchase decision.

Because of my recent experience, I've determined that you can learn as much, if not more, from certain "don'ts" than you can from certain "do's."

1. Manufacturers must keep apprised of, and periodically inspect, the quality of a re-sellers' operations. My "Greek tragedy" could have/should have been prevented.
2. Warranty claims departments must be operationally efficient. This is where problem solving can strengthen loyalty. The only burden borne by the affluent customer should be proof of purchase.
3. Empower problem solving: My frustration escalated out of control when I was told to fork over $650, despite proving that the warranty was valid for another 12 months. Absorbing the service charge and developing a loyal customer should be common sense, but alas, it's not common practice.
4. Learn to communicate with the affluent: Neither IBM (Lenovo) Warranty Service personnel nor the supervisors and staff remedied the situation to my satisfaction. Everyone moved from confusion to defensiveness to belligerence. Needless to say, these attitudes don't "cut it" with the affluent.

Having advised everyone from financial services professionals and luxury real-estate firms to high-end retailers and auctioneering firms, I've discovered that, although there are distinct and obvious differences in every industry, the affluent remain a constant. In other words, with slight, industry-specific modifications, my advice is applicable to nearly every product and service provider.

Probably the biggest mistake made by marketers of higher-ticket products and services is taking affluent consumers for granted. This is another way of saying that they don't understand the affluent. As result, they *don't* approach the affluent in the proper way, and at right times and places. Instead, they rely on costly ad campaigns and brochures to attract affluent clients and customers. But as I've pointed out, research demonstrates that top-quintile income earners are highly skeptical of advertising claims and promises.

The affluent want *proof* of quality and caring—via positive word-of-mouth from someone they trust and respect, the actions of the salesperson on the floor, or the manner they're greeted on the phone. The affluent are on the lookout for any disconnect between what they have heard and what they experience. They've been duped before, and don't want it to happen again. For each year that passes, and as affluent marketing heats up, their skepticism of marketing promises increases. Therefore, it's essential to offer high-quality products and personalized service, delivered when and where they want. It's also essential that you do *not* mislead your prospects.

Nobody is Indispensable

You are not the only person selling laptops, luxury cars, jewelry, condominiums or wealth management services. As Winston Churchill once said, "Men who think of themselves as indispensable are almost always wrong." Translation: affluent consumers *can* live without your product or service, and if they really want it, they *can* get it elsewhere. Your job is to convince them otherwise. Some reasons an affluent prospect will buy from you may include:

- Time savings.
- Aggravation savings.
- Highly personal service.
- Pampering that goes above and beyond the norm (reaching even "mind-blowing proportions).
- They've come to know you, like you and trust you.
- High-quality products or services.
- Status.

Let's re-cap the reasons the affluent might select a product or service, and compare them to my IBM experience.

Time savings: My time was wasted by both the reseller, IBM, and Lenovo.

Aggravation savings: My initial reason for purchasing the laptop from a local retailer was to eliminate the aggravation experienced with laptops previously purchased online, but I experienced *even more* aggravation from these particular sellers.

Highly Personal Service: This was a cruel joke.

Pampering Beyond the Norm: Given what a serious marketing issue this can be, my laptop experience was laughable. In my case, both the sellers and customer service personnel demonstrated ZERO understanding of the affluent.

Knowing, Liking and Trusting: I didn't know the reseller prior to my purchase, but I've bought IBM (Lenovo) computers in the past. Now that I really *know* them, I don't like or trust the manufacturer or its retailers. How's that for word-of-mouth influence?

High-Quality Products and Services: The product (my laptop) was trouble from Day One, as was the horrible warranty service with which I'm still struggling.

Status: So much for having a local computer guru. My word-of-mouth influence is now directed toward selling memberships at Costco.

First Contact

You must also realize that nobody will discover reasons to buy from *you* if you DON'T make first contact.

> Fifty top-ranked sales professionals spent an entire day together at a seminar. The seminar was held in a room within 100 feet of a doll auction. The auction was attended by hundreds of affluent prospects. Many dollars changed hands that day. Several attendees paid up to $40,000 for one doll. The auctioneers received between 10 and 35 percent of the sale price.

Not one top-ranked sales professional who targets the affluent attended the auction. These sales professionals need to ask themselves, "Is it more productive to cluster with high concentration of my competitors or with high concentrations of prospects.[37]

Do's

Not long ago, I was in Anchorage, Alaska to deliver lectures for several days. On the Sunday I arrived, I decided to explore downtown Anchorage. On spotting a Nordstrom's, I wandered inside to the men's department, where I was greeted by Sam, the department's Sunday salesman. Low-key, amiable and well-dressed, he asked, "Are you looking for anything in particular?" Truth be told, I wasn't, but then it occurred to me that I needed a new suit.

"Do you have any good Italian suits on sale?" I asked.

Even though this was a Nordstrom's, the last place I expected to find a high-end Italian suit (and on sale) was in Anchorage.

"I've got a beautiful Zegna that I picked up in Seattle," said Sam. "I think it's your size and it's marked down 50%. Let me show it to you."

The next thing I knew, Sam and his tailor were fitting me into a beautiful, navy Zegna two-piece suit. It needed only minor alterations, and Sam told me that he'd have it altered by the following morning and personally deliver it to my hotel. I left Nordstrom's that Sunday as the proud owner of a new Zegna suit!

When I returned from my speech the following afternoon, the suit was hanging in my hotel room closet. A week later, I received a call on my cell from Sam (he'd asked for the best way to contact me) to inquire how the suit fit. It fit perfectly, and I expressed my appreciation for his professionalism and follow-up. He laughed. "Just doing my job, and my job is to serve my customers. I love people, I love fine clothes, and with your permission, since I've got your size on record, and I'll stay on the lookout for quality bargains."

[37] Stanley, Dr. Thomas J., "Selling to the Affluent." McGraw-Hill, 1991, pp. 8–9.

Because he epitomized the art of selling to the affluent, I sent Sam a copy of my book of that same title. After receiving it, he called to thank me, and said it was one of the nicest things a customer had ever done for him. We chatted for a few minutes, and I soon discovered that Sam was one of Nordstrom's top salespeople—nationwide. This came as no surprise to me.

To date, I've purchased four Zegna suits from Sam. He's now my personal fashion consultant, some 7,000 miles away.

Lessons from the Do's—Consultative Selling

In Sam's case, I did *not* enter his sales environment expecting to purchase a suit. I was merely curious about the merchandise available in the Anchorage Nordstrom's. Anyway, let's walk through the reasons that Sam made it so easy for me to buy from him.

Time Savings: On a Sunday afternoon in Anchorage, when I had nothing else to do, Sam not only filled the void, but had a suit tailored and delivered to my room in less than 24 hours.

Aggravation savings: Sam was consultative, inquisitive, and involved (having the suit tailored so *I* wouldn't have get that done), thus allowing me to "get sold" myself.

Highly Personal Service: Nothing beats having a salesperson hand-deliver the product. A smile crossed my face as soon as I saw the suit in my closet.

Pampering Beyond the Norm: Sam pampered me with fast tailoring and by providing the service at no extra charge—even though the suit was discounted by 50%. As an extra topping on the "sundae," he personally delivered it to my room.

Knowing, Liking and Trusting: It didn't take long to know and like Sam. His actions quickly led to a high degree of trust.

High-Quality Products: I wanted a high-end Italian suit, and found one. This is an area where I splurge, because when delivering speeches and presentations worldwide, I want to look and feel my best.

Status: This wasn't a conscious reason for entering Nordstrom's, but it may have been at work on a subconscious level. This store and its merchandise ooze status.

Fear and Loathing on the Sales Floor

As a rule, the affluent are distrustful of salespeople and selling. Therefore, it's usually necessary to "make your pitch" in a subtle fashion—to sell without appearing to be a salesman. Instead, you must present the prospective client, one who already knows, likes and trusts you, with an opportunity. The idea is to be helpful and consultative.

Many salespeople go too far in one direction or the other instead of developing the correct balance between personal and business relationships. Sam asked very little about my personal life, although he did inquire about what brought me to Anchorage. It's not that he didn't want more personal information: his instincts told him that the timing wasn't right.

If you're thinking, "This all seems simple," you're right: it *is* simple. There's nothing complicated about selling to the affluent, *provided* you overcome any emotional, attitudinal and/or behavioral impediments. Unfortunately, such impediments frequently form the foundation of various avoidance tactics.

Top 5 Pitfalls

1. **"I am NOT a Salesman."** In the legal and financial services realm, for example, many people deny or denigrate the importance of actively recruiting new clients—*of selling.* "Salesman" is a dirty word, tantamount to prostitution. In the automobile business, the worst insult is to be called a "used car salesman." And that phrase has become an insult toward salespeople in general. But this doesn't have to be your reality. Regardless of the title printed on your business card, selling is *not* beneath you. It's a key component of your job. And if your salesmanship is consultative, it becomes seamless and you'll never be tarred

with the same brush as a used-car salesman. Everyone must raise his or her game, because *everyone* is targeting the affluent and the emerging affluent. But to win affluent business, you must get them to like you, trust you and respect you as a professional.

2. **Avoidance Patterns (Low-Impact "Busywork").** Social self-consciousness often leads people to use low-impact activities that keep affluent prospects at arm's length. Social self-consciousness involves feelings of intimidation in the presence of people of wealth, power and influence. Most of those suffering from social self-consciousness have an inferiority complex. At some level, they've decided that affluent people are their economic and social "betters." As a result, they feel uncomfortable associating with wealthy prospects, much less trying to sell to them. If not recognized and addressed, it will create avoidance patterns. Whenever these avoidance patterns are allowed to linger for any length of time, low-impact busywork develops into a bad habit. This can become a serious affliction for salespeople who are asked to deal with the affluent.

   Hal worked the sales floor of a high-end electronics company. Like most of his colleagues, he was a gadget geek and frustrated musician. *Unlike* his counterparts, Hal was so goal-focused on up-selling, that "even when affluent customers came in and stated, with conviction, that they knew what they were talking about, and wanted a specific flat-screen plasma TV for $2,500, nine out of ten times, they would walk out of the store after spending more than triple what they expected. But most of our salespeople are scared of affluent clients, selling them exactly what they ask for, and it's a lose-lose-lose: the customer doesn't get what he really needs, the salesperson doesn't earn a good commission, and the store doesn't generate the number of high-end sales that it could."

3. **Focusing on Image Rather than Substance.** Mastering the presentation without mastering the product will rarely pass the

affluent consumer's highly evolved "sniff-test" for being sold. The superficiality becomes much too transparent.

Some salespeople defer to the supposed selling power of PowerPoint presentations, brochures, websites and other collateral materials. They rely on marketing departments; they hire consultants to teach them to write 82-word elevator speeches and vague value propositions.

More often than not, they end up with slick brochures boasting about their processes and products, and their presentations come off as nothing but sizzle without the steak. The prospect sits there, thinking "Huh? What's this guy talking about?" Then he mentally tattoos a big "S" onto the person's forehead—which stands for "stupid" and/or "salesperson."

Hal possessed an encyclopedic knowledge of electronics, but rarely used it. Instead, he asked questions about the type of room in which prospects wanted to install their units, the layout of their houses, other entertainment considerations, etc. He would only get technical when forced to explain something in more detail, and then, "I always expanded the purchase."

Meanwhile, his peers sold the affluent exactly what they asked for, and did so only after regurgitating every advertised fact about a particular unit. This useless product information never led to an expanded purchase.

The affluent need to be aware of features and benefits, but they also need to be informed in a way they understand. That understanding, at least in their minds, needs to be clear and complete.

4. **Paralyzed by Preparation.** "If I could just read one more book, attend one more class, create another new brochure, fine-tune my PowerPoint presentation, *then* I'd be really prepared to prospect." Not really. People afflicted with preparation paralysis always think they need to learn more, work on the perfect presentation, or wait for the perfect brochure. This is another avoidance behavior that stems from fear.

Whenever we assess salespeople for social self-consciousness, whether it is luxury home sales, high-end automotive, financial services, or home security and entertainment, two of the most common afflictions scored are:

- I have set goals for attracting affluent prospects, but I haven't begun prospecting that group yet.
- I need and want to raise the bar so I can target affluent investors, but I really feel stuck.

The best salesperson does her homework and gathers "intelligence," but she's also flexible enough to respond to unexpected questions and situations—she is not afraid to take action under the pressure of the skeptical affluent consumer.

5. **It's *Never* the Right Moment.** This person can never find an appropriate "opening" that lets him steer the conversation toward business. There's always—always—a "valid" reason for not focusing on the sale. Sam is a salesman who could have assumed, "This guy's from the 'Lower 48.' He's not going to buy a suit today." But Sam isn't a typical salesperson. He understands that there's *never a perfect time*, never a perfect setting or place, and his job as a consultative salesperson means helping affluent customers and prospects make serious buying decisions.

More Overlooked Opportunities

Because 93% of today's affluent are self-made individuals—and many are business owners and salespeople, too—they're inclined to be achievement-oriented and respond to appeals to their achievements and status as successful businesspeople—not to their sense of class of affluence.

The enlightened sales professional looks for opportunities to associate his product or service with career achievements of the prospect. Some of the more innovative marketers of expensive products have discovered the value of the affluent business owner's need to own the symbols of achievement. A manufacturer of expensive watches gives the Rolex Spirit of Enterprise award each year to those whose accomplishments deserve special recognition.[38]

But as Dr. Thomas J. Stanley points out in *Selling to the Affluent*, few marketers and salespeople ever consider the benefits of incorporating their prospects' achievements into their pitches. Few bother to contact affluent prospects when they've just been recognized by their industry, community or a charitable organization. Sending a short, handwritten note to the businesswoman who just donated $10,000 to the local library can be an excellent way of opening the door to a relationship that may bear fruit in terms of immediately sales, as well as personal introductions and referrals. Yet Stanley was (and I am) shocked at the number of otherwise savvy salespeople who never take advantage of such opportunities.

In addition, I'm always surprised at the number of salespeople who spend breakfasts, lunches, golf outings and other social occasions exclusively in the company of their colleagues, rather than using the time to get to know affluent prospects. If you're spending most of your lunches with your buddies from the 15th floor, then you're wasting most of your lunches. A true rainmaker is either devoting her time to providing higher quality (and more personalized service) to existing clients, or she's on the phone, at her computer or outside the office making personal connections with new, affluent prospects.

While we're on the subject of opportunities, never forget that women should be a prime target for marketers. Research tells us that they have a major influence in big purchase decisions (more statistically significant than males), and with regard to finances, women are more likely than men to want their financial health to be in order. They want clarity, convenience and value. It is important, therefore, for marketers to earn the trust of affluent women. They are more loyal than men, and they aggressively stimulate word-of-mouth influence. Focus

---

[38] Ibid, p. 12.

on beauty, finances, health, family, security, convenience, children (grandchildren) and travel.

Many firms now hire more women in sales and marketing roles, and rightfully so. As I indicated above, women control much of major decision making—especially relative to coordinating and overseeing their family's financial affairs. Therefore, the financial advisor meeting with a husband *and* a wife increases the probability of selling a complete package of services than when meeting with the husband alone. And when *women* meet with husband and wife combos, this further increases the probability of a big sale.

Create a Warm Sales Environment

This is a *common sense* principle that's not always common practice. As we have already discussed, today's mature boomers are hard-working and highly stressed. Whenever you can make them feel comfortable during the sales process, you accelerate the probability of a transaction. Top sales professionals understand this, and go to great lengths to provide personal service through every stage of the buying experience. They would never consider delivering lip service, even when their instincts tell them that a particular shopper is not serious. Always be sincere, discuss product benefits that you know are real, never make a promise you can't keep or a statement whose accuracy you aren't certain about, and whenever possible, over-deliver on every aspect of the sales process.

Whether you are working out of your home, your car, whether you are in a retail environment, or your work takes you inside the home of affluent prospects and clients, you can create a sales environment that is warm, friendly and inviting. Regardless of environmental factors outside of your control, you can impact any environment by viewing it as an extension of your personality and professional image. We are all sources of energy, and because most affluent consumers are stressed and don't like the sales process, your energy must be extremely positive—such that it exercises a subtle calming influence on the consumer.

Everything and everybody contributes to your sales environment.

This includes different personnel and the forms of communication you use to establish and maintain contact—including the phone, email or regular mail. You must be aware of all these contact points, recognize strengths and weaknesses, and work to make the overall experience and overall sales environment as customer friendly as possible.

There are often times when appearances can be deceiving. I know of a local deli that's always packed with affluent customers, with a line that often winds from the cash register to the front door. The floors are old cold tile, the place is noisy, tables are nothing special, silverware is plastic, and drinks are served in Styrofoam cups. Yet this "greasy spoon" creates an affluent-friendly environment. The waiters and waitresses are extremely fast and friendly, the owner works the grill to help fill orders, and any problem is resolved immediately. I'll bet you know of a place or two like this.

Contrast that deli with an upscale steakhouse I recently visited during my travels. Within 20 minutes of being seated for dinner, my party of four was getting antsy. Although the restaurant had invested a tremendous amount to create a warm and upscale environment, our hostess was not very friendly—a flaw that would have been overlooked had we enjoyed a superior dining experience. But after waiting 20 minutes for a server, and because I was catching flight later that evening, I informed our "so-so" hostess that we had yet to be visited by a waiter. Although the food was fine, the service was anything but excellent. In fact, thanks to my complaint, we received service with an attitude, not a smile.

People make or break a sales environment, whether it's a greasy spoon, a high-end restaurant, or a tech person installing your home entertainment/security system. Being responsive, friendly, and customer/client-centric are key components in developing and preserving a warm sales environment.

I visit scores of establishments catering to the affluent—medical offices, upscale retail stores, upscale malls, bulk purchase outlets, airports, automobile dealerships, restaurants, hotels, bank offices and financial services firms—and the most successful are very nice: inside and out. If your reception area has room for just a few chairs, make sure the magazines are current; make certain you have a good relationship with the receptionist, and be sure the receptionist knows who you're expecting. Regardless of how well appointed an office might appear, it will never offset the irritation caused by keeping an affluent prospect or client/customer waiting for very long.

A Word on Feedback

Your affluent clients want good service, they want it on their terms, and they want to be heard. It is important to have a built in feedback-loop so your clients get the feeling that you want to hear from them. The easier you make it for an affluent client to contact you—and if not you, some other person who will listen to them and/or solve a problem –the more likely you are to strengthen their loyalty to you and your firm.

Client satisfaction surveys can be helpful if employed properly by your home office, but they are often perceived by affluent consumers as a nuisance. Whenever possible, you want to make this communication personal.

Salespeople who enjoy the most success with the affluent are the ones that develop close working relationships with their clients, serving as relationship managers and keeping their finger on the pulse of needs, wants and comments. They keep their antenna out, looking for ways to improve. Whether that improvement involves a product or something related to service—good sales people know.

Ask, Listen and *Then* Respond

A vital skill is the ability to ask good questions. Questions can do more to establish your competence than any statement. Questions draw out valuable information and opinions that you can use to personalize your response and whatever you are planning to present. Questions convince people that you're truly interested in them.

To successfully cater to the affluent, you must also become a good listener. That means really listening! Don't start thinking about your response, or you'll miss something important. Take notes, when appropriate. Ask for further clarification. Nod your head and give short acknowledgements such as, "That's great," "You must be proud of that," "That's helpful to know."

Practice incorporating what you've heard into your responses and anything you present later. Use phrases such as, "You mentioned that . . .", "Since you stated that __________ is important to you . . ." or "You asked about . . ." Or, in Sam's case "Are you looking for anything in particular?"

Your responses needn't be fancy, but sincere questions are great persuaders and relationship builders. And *every* facet of selling to the affluent revolves around establishing and maintaining healthy relationships!

Think in terms of your recent interactions as an affluent consumer, and recall the lessons of this chapter:

- Environment.
- Quality of the product you were purchasing.
- Level of personalized service you received.
- Aggravation savings.
- Time savings.
- Pampering.
- Salesperson's knowledge, likeability and trustworthiness.
- Cachet of the entire experience.

Chart 8-1					
Rate Your Last Purchase Experience					
	Bad				**Excellent**
1. The sales environment was warm, friendly, and helpful.	1	2	3	4	5
2. The quality of the products (services) purchased was outstanding.	1	2	3	4	5
3. I received very professional and complete personalized service.	1	2	3	4	5
4. My purchase and post-purchase experience was completely free of aggravation.	1	2	3	4	5
5. My purchase experience was very time-efficient.	1	2	3	4	5
6. I felt pampered throughout the entire purchase experience.	1	2	3	4	5
7. The sales and service personnel were knowledgeable, friendly and exuded trustworthiness.	1	2	3	4	5
8. I actually enjoyed the purchase experience.	1	2	3	4	5

Scoring Key

36–40: Fantastic! You're about to become a raving fan, if you're not already.
30–35: Good job. With a few adjustments needed.
27–34: Average.
<27: Poor

Research Facts

- Solving problems quickly, communicating clearly, and ensuring that your client or customer is satisfied are the top criteria for strengthening the loyalty of your affluent clients. —2004 APD research
- Personalized service is a close second when it comes to strengthening affluent client/customer loyalty. —2004 APD research
- Affluent women are the major decision makers in family purchase decisions. —2007 Understanding the Affluent research
- The affluent do not like feeling that they are being sold. —2004 APD research; 2007 Understanding the Affluent research

9

Ritz Carlton Service + FedEx Efficiency

When determining whether to use a product/service provider again, price was among the lowest priorities cited by the affluent.

— Factoid, 2004 Affluent Purchasing Decision research study

A few years ago, a business coach ("Jeffrey") decided to mix pleasure with business. After conducting seminars in the Los Angeles area, he arranged for his wife Lois to spend the weekend with him at the Pasadena Ritz Carlton. Days before Lois departed for L.A., she received a call from "Karen," a member of the concierge staff at the Club Level, who asked if the couple had any special requests. Lois said that since her husband would be picking her up at LAX at 9:30 on Saturday morning, she'd love an early check-in. Karen said she'd look into it, and asked if this was a special occasion. Lois told her that it was their anniversary ("which it was . . . in a spiritual sense").

When they arrived at the hotel at 10:00 on Saturday morning, Karen showed them to the Club Level and said they'd been upgraded to a room with a better view. She also introduced them to Juan, who was in charge of the Club Level during the day. Jeffrey asked what time the Club Level opened on Sunday morning, and was visibly disappointed when Juan said it opened at 7:00. Jeffrey figured there was no way he could wait that long for a cup of coffee. So Jeffrey asked where the closest Starbucks was and what time it opened. There was a Starbucks a few blocks away, but Juan thought the store also opened at 7:00.

After spending time at the beach that afternoon, Jeffrey and Lois visited the hotel's spa. When they returned to the room, they encountered a delightful surprise. There was a coffee pot, a basket of Starbucks coffees and two Ritz Carlton mugs. Inside one of the mugs was a handwritten note from Juan that read: "Happy anniversary and welcome to the Ritz Carlton. I hope you will find what you need to have coffee when you wake up tomorrow morning. Please keep the cups to remember your visit with us this weekend." Jeffrey was blown away. He never dreamed that Juan would go to all the trouble to buy coffee, and provide a coffee pot and mugs. After Lois examined the basket, she realized that there was enough coffee to last for weeks. Juan's gift was not inexpensive, and Jeffrey was really impressed. He decided right then to let the management of the hotel know what a positive impression Juan and Karen had made.

For Jeffrey, *that* was extraordinary service—a model he won't soon forget when it comes to serving his own affluent clients.[39]

Contrast Jeffrey's service experience with Gerald's attempt to test drive a new Lexus. Just as the Ritz Carlton has become the benchmark for service in the hospitality world, Lexus has earned a similar reputation for luxury automobiles. Gerald, one of America's top-quintile income earners, has owned and driven luxury cars for over 25 years. Because of positive word-of-mouth and *Consumer Reports* reviews, Gerald decided to test-drive a Lexus GS 350.

Like most affluent consumers, Gerald had done his homework, knew the price points and options, and just wanted to experience the car. This meant, naturally, that he wanted a test drive. On his lunch hour, he visited a local dealer, where he was warmly greeted by a seemingly "senior" salesman. Gerald explained that he merely wanted to take a quick test drive, and had about 30 minutes. The salesman

[39] Adapted from *Rising Star* by Cordell Parvin and Kristi Sebalj. Dallas: Life Career Publishing, 2007.

listened, said he would get someone to help, and walked away. A minute later, a young salesman appeared, and asked Gerald to repeat the request he'd just made. Obviously, "senior" did not communicate anything to "junior," other than directing him to Gerald, who now—three minutes into his experience—thought, "I'm annoyed." Not a good sign.

Maybe the young salesman was nervous, maybe he wasn't trained properly, but he wasn't listening to Gerald. He kept asking specific questions about the features he wanted and then explaining those features during his time-crunched lunch hour—features Gerald wasn't the least bit interested in hearing about, since he'd already done his homework. In desperation, Gerald finally blurted out, "I only have 10 minutes left to drive the car. All I want is to drive it. You don't need to sell me; you don't need to talk about your service. I know it's great. The car will either sell or un-sell itself."

According to Gerald, this made the salesperson even more nervous. He went inside to get a license plate, which took another couple of minutes, and as they finally approached a new GS 350, Gerald was informed that he was not allowed to drive it until the salesman demonstrated the car by driving it off the lot.

As the salesman drove down the road, and continued to explain the finer features, Gerald replied, "I've been driving luxury cars for 25 years, and I'm sure today's models all have comparable paint and windshields—I just want to drive the car!"

When he finally drove the car, Gerald soon turned it around toward the dealership, explaining that it was a nice car, but didn't "wow" him. Gerald then asked for the range of lease packages—something the salesperson was incapable of immediately providing.

Needless to say, Gerald did not return to the dealership. He's driving a new Mercedes, having spent more money than if he'd selected the Lexus.

This isn't meant as a backhanded slap at Lexus: they do an excellent job of attracting, serving and developing loyal affluent clients. In Gerald's case, however, a confluence of human errors showcased Lexus' products and services in a poor light.

As it turns out, the senior salesman was actually the sales manager. He was trying to give the young salesman some experience and (maybe) a sale. But because neither salesperson listened to Gerald's *single* request, the car "had to completely WOW me to compensate for my annoyance."

The lesson is clear: having an outstanding product with a reputation for superior service is not enough in a crowded and competitive marketplace—especially when you're dealing with the affluent.

The Affluent Litmus Test

FedEx has created superior standards for service and especially for operational efficiency. Because so many of today's affluent are self-employed or high-powered corporate managers, they regularly employ overnight carriers such as the UPS, Airborne Express or DHL. For my money, however, FedEx is the one and only "gold standard" by which all others are judged. If I absolutely, positively need packages to arrive at their destinations on time, I rely on FedEx.

Ritz-Carlton service and FedEx efficiency are the litmus test by which the affluent will judge you and your organization. This requires that your company not only supply high-quality products and services, but that your employees are fully engaged and fully committed to customer service—during and after the sale. The Oechsli Institute's 2004 research study, *How the Affluent Make Purchasing Decisions*, revealed that affluent Americans place the highest priority on service. When it comes to determining whether to use the same product/service provider for a second time, the affluent made their decisions based on whether:

1. Any problems encountered were resolved quickly and satisfactorily.
2. The company provided good service following the purchase.
3. The company provided the information needed to make a sound purchase decision.
4. Their guarantees of satisfaction were clearly defined.

5. Preferred brands were available through the retailer.
6. The people representing the company were friendly and helpful.
7. They offered the lowest price available.

Note the lower priority given to price vs. quality service, problem resolution, clearly defined guarantees and helpful employees. Again, this isn't because America's top quintile is looking to get "ripped off" in terms of price. They aren't. The affluent are always on the lookout for good deals. But for most of them, a "good deal" has more to do with pre-purchase and post-purchase experiences provided by the sellers than the costs of the products/services alone.

Full Commitment

Although the affluent recognize that not everything is within your control—"lemons" sometimes sneak past quality control and employees sometimes have "bad days"—they expect you to have policies and procedures to ensure total satisfaction. And they expect you to take the lead in remedying problems with the merchandise or services that you sell. If the affluent are not completely satisfied with the product and their purchase experience, there can be no "buck passing." America's wealthiest consumers expect that *you*, the manager or business owner, will get *personally* involved to *successfully* resolve any grievances they may have in the shortest possible timeframe.

Recall the story of Harold and Maude from Chapter 3. If John, the accountant and tax preparer, had immediately responded to Harold's complaints regarding his state and federal returns—had he volunteered to pick up the forms and return corrected versions with 24 hours, John might have acquired a new customer willing to overlook his initial blunders, and then recommend his services to affluent friends and family members. Instead, John's attitude displayed a complete disinterest in whether Harold became a repeat customer or not. Obviously, John was not familiar with the following:

A study by Bain & Company in Boston found that successful companies have two common traits: a high percentage of repeat business and low levels of employee turnover. Regardless of size, the companies studied were vastly more profitable than their competitors. Their leaders know that loyalty—internal and external—is a better profit forecaster than market share, cost position or quality of service. If you want higher profits, therefore, aim for employee loyalty.[40]

Hiring the Right Staff

Many people working with an affluent clientele hire people to assist them in delivering Ritz-Carlton service combined with FedEx efficiency, but too often, retailers and high ranking sales professionals try to fill slots with the first "decent" candidates who wander into the office. Do *not* hire people who are merely looking for a job. Your path to success with the affluent is to build long-term relationships, and you can't do that with today's typical job seeker. When you talk about your business and your goals with job candidates, you need to carefully watch for evidence that potential hires are becoming visibly excited about being part of that vision.

> Employee disengagement and turnover are the inevitable results of mismatching people to jobs, people to companies and people to people. The term "human resources" is misleading. Just because humans are working for you doesn't mean you have resources. For people to be productive, they must believe in themselves and their contributions. People must also believe that their talents and personalities are compatible with the job and their co-workers.
>
> [It's] a process that begins *before* the applicant is hired. It starts when you match the right people with the right positions, and continues when you put the focus on people—when you manage people with an eye toward helping them achieve their goals so they can achieve those of your organization. Ultimately, it's about producing a symbiotic relationship between

---

[40] Kabachnick, Terri, *I Quit, But Forgot to Tell You.* Largo, FL: The Kabachnick Group, Inc., 2006, pp. 17–18.

> the manager and the managed, the company and the employee—fostering an environment in which everybody wins, and nobody loses.[41]

As I wrote in *The Art of Selling to the Affluent,* "There are certain tasks associated with any position, and you must be certain that applicants have the attitudes, knowledge, abilities, experience, and skills to perform all of those tasks with a high level of competence. But that's just the beginning. The only people who will last in your Ritz-Carlton service environment are those with superior customer service skills. Here are the qualities you need to explore:

- "*Caring:* They must care enough about providing extraordinary customer service that they will do whatever is necessary to provide it, either directly or by going out of their way to serve other employees at any level to help them serve a customer or client.
- "*Friendly:* Being friendly when they are in the right mood, got a good night's sleep, and are being treated kindly by others is not sufficient. Their friendly attitude must weather almost any storm and shine through.
- "*Attentive:* Everyone is attentive, but many focus that attention inward. You need people who are outwardly attentive, constantly aware of other people's needs and looking for ways to meet those needs.
- "*Energetic:* I see this as energy that is constantly moving toward the point of need. Some high-energy people never seem to focus, and that is not what you want.
- "*Confident:* Confident people do not brag or fish for compliments. They simply step up and do what needs to be done. When complimented for it, they simply say 'Thank you,' and keep doing it.
- "*Never satisfied:* The benchmarks of Ritz-Carlton-level service require people who are never satisfied. When this quality is com-

[41] Ibid, p. 109.

bined with the other five, you have a person who will help you make things happen in a big way.

- "*Professional:* Whether you are valet parking your car, visiting the health club/spa, or checking into your room, everyone at the Ritz-Carlton is extremely professional. This is no accident. They are trained to serve all guests with the utmost professionalism.

"You can detect these qualities during a hiring interview. List each quality on the left side of a legal pad, leaving space between each for notes, then keep the following cues in mind.

- "As you observe individuals during the interview, you will see indications that they are or are not *friendly*, *attentive*, and *energetic*. Write down the specific cues that you observe.
- "To explore the *caring* quality, explain that caring for the needs of customers and other employees is an important aspect of the position they are seeking. Ask them to give you specific instances from previous jobs or other situations where they gave special care for customers, fellow employees, or other people. As they respond, make notes on what they did. Hold off evaluating what they say until later. If they overlook caring for customers and/or fellow employees, ask again for an example.
- "To explore their *confidence*, give them examples of the kinds of tasks they will be performing if they are hired. Give them one example at a time and ask them how they would accomplish that task. Listen for and write down cues relating to their confidence level. Make special note of any comments they make about 'not being sure' or explaining the steps they would take to prepare for doing that task.
- "Testing the *never satisfied* quality is challenging. Explain what you are currently doing in a specific area to meet the expectations of your customers or clients. Then ask them how they think this could be improved. After they have given you their suggestions, ask them if they would then be satisfied that they were doing everything they could to delight customers/clients. Note their response.

- Have they done their homework? Researching your business, knowing your corporate strategy, vision, and specific objectives is a signal of someone who takes initiative. Whenever a candidate researches your competition, they have just taken this initiative to the next level.

Keeping the Right Staff

"It's that long-term relationship with customers or clients issue again. If you've gone to the trouble to hire the right people, it only makes sense to work hard to keep them. Even in tough economic times when jobs are difficult to come by, people with the preceding qualities are highly valued. If you don't work hard to keep the right people, they will be the first to leave. The question is: What do you have to do to keep them? We tackle that question at two levels:

1. "The *job context* level: These are the things that must be present to *prevent job dissatisfaction.* They include the following:
   a. They must believe that their compensation and benefits are *adequate* enough for them to meet their personal and family financial obligations.
   b. They must believe *equity* exists when they compare their compensation and benefits with what people in comparable positions receive—people within and outside the organization.
   c. They must believe there is *opportunity* for promotion within the organization to the level and types of positions to which they aspire.
   d. They must believe that the *expectations, support,* and *feedback* they receive from their immediately supervisor are fair, adequate, and consistent.
   e. They must enjoy people and have *complete belief* in the value of your product or services.

2. "The *job content* level: These are the things that must exist in order to provide the motivation to continually improve performance. They include the following:
   a. They must *believe in* and be *committed* to the *organization's purpose and goals.*
   b. They must clearly see how what they do each day *contributes to achieving organizational goals.*
   c. They must genuinely *enjoy performing the tasks* associated with their position.
   d. They must have the *freedom to perform their tasks* without unnecessary interference from policies, procedures, rules, practices and tight supervision.
   e. They must have the *ability to reduce or eliminate* policies, procedures, rules, practices and tight supervision that prevent them from successfully performing their tasks.
   f. They must have an opportunity to *figure things out* and *make decisions.*
   g. They must receive *adequate and ongoing training* that enables them to continually improve their performance.
   h. *Risk taking* must be encouraged and rewarded, especially when they fail."
   i. They must truly enjoy *helping* affluent prospects and customer / clients make purchase decisions.
   j. They must become *students* of the affluent.

Creating and Improving Processes

Terms such as "buy in," "stakeholder" and "ownership" have become clichés in corporate America, largely because many owners and managers using the terms insist on creating, revising and imposing processes from the *top down* for individual departments or their companies as a whole, with little or no input from employees. In my view, this is a colossal mistake. Processes should always be created, monitored and improved by the people charged with performing them. This is the only way an organization can provide consistent, high-quality services to customers and clients.

This requires, of course, that business owners and managers understand how every department and division operates within the organization—from the perspective of the "grunts" on the front lines. An "ivory tower" solution to a set of customer-service problems may have zero to do with reality unless management theorists get down into the trenches with the employees. For small businesses, this may mean spending a few days with the sales force, customer-service reps and accounts receivable. For a larger organization, the learning process will (obviously) require more time.

In Chapter 7, I mentioned a friend who once worked for a major metropolitan newspaper. That newspaper was *The New York Times*, where my friend witnessed something unusual—something that left a lasting impression on him as a businessman.

Before Arthur Sulzberger, Jr. was handed the reins of the "newspaper of record," the previous publisher (his father) insisted that the young man be fully immersed—for months at a time, in some cases—in nearly every department responsible for producing a modern newspaper. This meant working and eating lunches with the ad salesmen, printers, truckers, reporters and editors. (My friend met him when he proposed a story for the "Metropolitan" Section, and Mr. Sulzberger actually approved—unlike many other editors—the kid's ideas for two articles.)

Since neither my friend nor I are current employees of the *Times*, we can't say that this "total immersion therapy" produced the desired results. But I'd be willing to bet that Mr. Sulzberger is much more attuned to the need for employee input regarding process development and refinement than he would have been if he'd been given the top spot without exposure to hundreds of employees.

Researching the Competition

As I wrote in *The Art of Selling to the Affluent*, whether you're selling services or products, the basic tenets of this detective work are the same. You must learn everything possible about your competition, both from your own perspective and that of the prospect—the competition's marketing promises, current ad campaigns, rebates, warranties, the quality of their product or service, their availability, technical differences, level of personal service and follow-through, etc. "You want to assess both their strengths and weaknesses. Here's a checklist that can assist you in getting started:

- Create a separate file folder for each competitor.
- Collect all current marketing, advertising, and promotional materials; special offerings, rebates, etc.
- Have someone other than you (a secret shopper) contact each competitor, expressing interest in their particular products or services.
- Create a script for each secret shopper to follow that includes questions about quality, service, availability, price and warranty. Make certain that your secret shopper takes accurate notes.
- If possible have your secret shopper ask for information to be mailed. You want to determine competitors' responsiveness and collect all possible collateral materials. The standard is FedEx Efficiency.
- Have your secret shoppers complete a form that includes a checklist to use in evaluating basic service issues, such as whether competitors were pleasant, accommodating, responsive, knowledgeable, and professional. The standard being Ritz-Carlton service.
- Whenever possible, determine the 'position' that your competitor holds in the mind of your affluent market."

You can add or subtract from this list as you see fit. The idea is to determine which of your competitors is best-in-class and why. From this platform of intelligence, you'll be able to create a personal benchmark that is tailored specifically to your business. As you complete each competitor evaluation, ask yourself: "Have I discovered anything new that will help me achieve a higher level of Ritz-Carlton service, backed by FedEx efficiency?" If your answer is yes, do something about it. According to our 2004 APD research, evaluating and comparing options has a significant impact in the final major purchase decision.

It is important to continually circle all of this back to your Ritz-Carlton Service and FedEx Efficiency. Why? Because these are two of the most statistically significant criteria the affluent use to differentiate between marketing hyperbole and reality. And mark my words, the affluent are reality based. They do not trust the hyperbole, because they've heard it all before. So one of the more important pieces of intelligence you will gather from studying the competition will come from your secret shopper.

It is here where you will get a true understanding of where your competition ranks regarding service. You want to know what your competitors do well in terms of servicing prospects, where they stumble, where you are superior, and what could you learn that could be applied to improve your service.

You also want to have an understanding of their operational efficiency. Again, you should always be striving to improve your efficiencies.

Research Facts

When it comes to determining whether to use the same product/service provider for a second time, the affluent made their decisions based on whether:

1. Any problems encountered were resolved quickly and satisfactorily.
2. The company provided good service following the purchase.
3. The company provided the information needed to make a sound purchase decision.
4. Their guarantees of satisfaction were clearly defined.
5. Preferred brands were available through the retailer.
6. The people representing the company were friendly and helpful.
7. They offered the lowest price available.

10

Communicating with the Affluent

No man ever listened himself out of a job.

—Calvin Coolidge

Personal communication with trusted family members, friends and colleagues has a major effect on affluent purchase decisions.

—2004 APD research

To me, the most shocking revelation from the Oechsli Institute's 2004–2005 research project *Attracting New Affluent Clients,* was the intense resistance and reluctance among many salespeople to do what it takes to succeed. Despite the technical platforms provided by their companies—high-end sales and marketing tools, cutting-edge products, personalized services, comprehensive warranties, etc.—a significant number of salespeople simply do not want to perform the necessary sales activities. And this holds true for people selling industrial products, landscaping and remodeling services, financial services, and all the other industries catering to affluent Americans.

Too many people hide behind jargon and a façade of expertise. In addition, many sales professionals talk too much, without saying anything. While the savvy salesperson builds relationships by asking strategic questions *and really listening,* the "wannabe" tries to impress prospects with multi-syllabic jargon to demonstrate how much he/she knows.

This produces two outcomes:

1. The affluent prospect walks away thinking, "That was painful. This guy's really impressed with himself." Or, "I'm totally confused . . ."
2. The ineffective salesperson walks away with absolutely NO INTELLIGENCE on the prospect, no insight that can be used for the purposes of consultative selling—which is the very opposite of what he or she should have done.

If you're serious about marketing and selling your products or services to the affluent, the good news is that it won't take long to distance yourself from the competition. On the other hand, be aware that even those who "walk the talk" frequently stumble. They make mistakes that could be easily avoided, as you're about to discover.

Most people think of landscaping as a weekly lawn-care service that might occasionally plant a few new bushes. And that's precisely how most of these outfits operate. But the most successful landscaping companies market and sell premium services in affluent neighborhoods. Every city has at least one high-end operation that's light-years ahead of the competition in every aspect—capabilities, service, performance, earnings and positive (affluent) word-of-mouth influence.

Take the Sullivans, please! They purchased a luxury home at a good price, albeit below market value, because it had been empty and neglected for over a year. Much of that neglect involved the yard—the house had poor curb appeal. Therefore, the Sullivans committed to using what they'd saved on the purchase price to paint the interior and landscape the yard. On the recommendation from a friend, Ms. Sullivan called the premier landscaping company in town and scheduled an appointment. The meeting lasted an hour, with Ms. Sullivan agreeing to pay $350.00 for this company to draw up a comprehensive "landscape design" for the entire yard. Within a week, she received the plans and a price range, depending on the plants and brickwork selected, with prices ranging from $28,400 to $37,950. The landscaping firm could start immediately, and the job would be completed within three weeks.

Because this was more than the $15,000 the Sullivans had originally budgeted, they decided to use the plans and meet with other landscapers. THIS is where the games began. Ms. Sullivan made copies of the landscape design created by the first company and met with three other landscapers, providing each with a copy of the plans. Each landscaper immediately claimed that they could do the job for considerably less money.

Two months later, after multiple interactions with each of the other firms, including meetings, no-show meetings, proposals, estimates, start and completion dates, unreturned phone calls and complete frustration, Ms. Sullivan contacted the original firm and gave the go-ahead for the project.

The lessons from the Sullivan's landscaping experience are a "must read" for any company attempting to attract, serve and develop a loyal affluent following. To keep from writing another book within this book, I'll merely highlight the obvious:

- Be Punctual—the only landscaping company that was consistently punctual in all of the Sullivan's dealings was the original—the one that eventually got the job. The others wasted Ms. Sullivan's time by either not showing up, or not returning phone calls in a timely manner.
- Listen Carefully—obviously, the winning landscaping firm listened carefully enough to create a full-scale landscape design. The others simply focused on the plan, without listening to Ms. Sullivan, who was not locked into that plan. After all, it was considerably above her budget.
- Asks Questions—this goes hand-in-hand with listening. Few questions were asked by the competitors, and most of their discussions revolved around their knowledge of plants, much of which went over Ms. Sullivan's head.
- Summarize—if the landscapers had taken the time to listen, question and then summarize what they'd heard, they would have significantly increased the probability of making a strong first impression.

- Follow-up—each of the losing bidders failed miserably when it came to following-up in a timely manner. In fact, one landscaper told her that he could not meet her on a Saturday because "I've got two children, and my weekends are devoted to family." It's hard to imagine a service company catering to the affluent that doesn't work on Saturdays.
- Professionalism—as you walk through these basic lessons, it's obvious that the losing bidders were not very professional. However, it took Ms. Sullivan two frustrating months to finally come to the same conclusion. Initially, she wanted to give them a chance, but in her words, "I wouldn't accept [these excuses] from my teenage son." The idea of professionalism is basic: be punctual and courteous, listen-question-summarize, explain what you'll do and DO exactly what you said.

The Financial Planner

These lessons apply to everyone attempting to market services to the affluent. Doug, a suit-and-tie professional, learned this the hard way. After finally arranging a face-to-face meeting with an affluent prospect, a businessman referred to him two months earlier, Doug became nervous. He'd carefully prepared for the meeting, since he felt this prospect would make an ideal client. But nothing went as planned, and it had nothing to do with his prospect. It was all about Doug.

Because of his nerves, Doug felt he needed to carry the conversation. So, as soon as they met, he began talking . . . and talking . . . and talking. While talking, Doug knew he should shut up, but for reasons he's still unable to articulate, he kept on talking. And we all know what happens when people talk too much: they focus on their favorite topic—themselves. Doug found himself making this cardinal sin.

Finally, in an attempt to force himself to stop talking, he pulled his "pitch" book out of this briefcase and started walking his affluent prospect through 48 pages of graphs, charts, and—from his prospect's perspective—financial confusion. Whether or not he was annoyed with Doug or seriously confused, he was courteous enough not to let on.

But actions always speak louder than words. Doug's prospect politely stopped in the middle of his pitch book, asking if he could take it with him, since this was a lot to digest at one sitting.

The meeting ended shortly thereafter. As soon as Doug's ideal prospect had the pitch book in his hands, he took complete control of the meeting by saying, "Thanks for the coffee. I'll give you a call after I've reviewed these materials." Doug tried to regain control by asking to set a time to meet again, but was brushed off with, "I'm going to be extremely busy. I know how to contact you." Doug knew this wasn't a good signal.

As a professional marketing his services to the affluent, Doug had done many things right. He had gotten a referral and persisted for two months until he was able to arrange a meeting. He carefully prepared for the meeting, though one might argue he was over-prepared. He simply lacked the communication skills to handle a face-to-face meeting with an affluent prospect. Doug's real problem was that he didn't truly understand the affluent. He was counting on his preparation and pitch book to impress and pave the way. But as Doug learned—the hard way—*he* is the product.

Circle back to the Sullivan's landscaping experience and the lessons learned, and we see that Doug failed on many of the same points as the landscapers. Because Doug talked too much and couldn't control his nerves, he didn't ask the right questions and didn't uncover opportunities to discuss his services, all of which negated any chance to summarize or schedule follow-up activities. After two months of pursuit, Doug lost this affluent prospect in less than an hour. Ouch!

Listen and Learn

Whether you sell landscaping services, high-end entertainment systems or financial services, you *must* ask questions that enable you to gather information and develop a rapport with your prospects and clients. Listen and learn so you can consider ways to provide real value to the person before attempting to discuss business, much less present your brochure.

The typical sales professional goes through a basic drill when meeting with a prospect. He takes total control (or so he thinks), and spends most of the time talking about himself, his products and services, how he delivers these products and services, and how professional and credible he is. In effect, he talks too much, listens too little, and fails to develop the skills necessary to begin transitioning the individual from prospect to client. All too frequently, like Doug, people attempt to communicate either by talking or by using collateral materials. Without making an effort to really know your prospect, there's no way you can position yourself as a solutions provider, a true professional who can add real value.

When you ask and listen in order to develop rapport, you really get to know a prospect. Say, for example, that you're a financial planner who discovers that a prospect has an ill mother and a sister who's about to lose her job. You can now talk about cash flow and suggest investments accordingly. You'll discover a wide range of likes and dislikes. You'll learn that this particular affluent prospect, Mr. Oechsli, really enjoys baseball because he grew up in New York and learned math by reading the box scores with his father. Knowing this, you decide to send him a *New York Times* photo book of historical baseball photographs. Since you are not a real baseball fan, the Internet and Amazon.com have enabled you to track down a rather unique baseball book and have it delivered to your prospect, complete with a note from you. Imagine Mr. Oechsli's surprise and delight at receiving this simple, but thoughtful, gift.

Just imagine if one of the losing landscapers had the presence of mind to uncover a passion point for Ms. Sullivan. It wouldn't have been very hard, as she had two Golden Retrievers at her side at all times as they walked through her yard. A couple of questions about the dogs would have uncovered her passion, "They're my big babies . . ." and a simple follow-up note, gift or coffee table book might not have guaranteed the business, but it would have made a serious and positive impact on Ms. Sullivan.

And incidentally, who do you think had the most influence over the Sullivan's landscaping decision. You guessed it: Ms. Sullivan.

If you want to become more successful in marketing your wares to the affluent you should always be thinking about the "coffee table book." What unique gift can you send to your prospect/client? To answer that question, you must learn enough about Mr. Oechsli to know he's a die-hard Atlanta Braves fan, went to school in Arizona, owns eight pairs of cowboy boots and a custom- made cowboy hat, and that he's an avid reader of history.

Ms. Sullivan is an animal lover who dotes on her Golden Retrievers. Further observation would uncover that she also enjoys wine (she has a small wine cellar in her basement), and is an aerobics instructor at a local health club. Any one of those interests may warrant the gift of a "coffee table book" with a personal note attached. It could really make a difference, because it's personal!

Many of these same skills apply to your best customers or clients as well. A simple but accurate marketing tactic is to view each of your top 25 customers or clients as being responsible for six new similar-profile customers or clients over the course of your professional relationship. In other words, affluent marketing success requires positive word-of-mouth influence. Call the client on her birthday, even if it's Sunday. Most people think they're beating the competition when they have an assistant mail a load of birthday cards. A top sales professional is always personal. And, of course, each client will receive your cell phone number and 24/7 access to your time. Right?

Ask the Right Questions

When it comes your time to talk, don't "pull a Doug" and talk-talk-talk. This is not communication! And don't tell the prospect everything you've ever learned about horticulture, high-definition plasma televisions or financial planning. Instead, maintain a conversational tone while you ask questions. Then use the answers to introduce your products and services. This can begin with a prospect inquiring about your services. Questions work both ways, as your prospective customers and clients will frequently ask you for information, both personal and specific. The secret is to always transition your responses into opportunities.

For instance, in response to being asked what he does for a living, one financial advisor I know responds with, "I work with a select group of families in the Chicago area, overseeing and coordinating their financial affairs." If his response leads to another question about his services, which is his desire, he continues with, "I do it very carefully. First I have to make a thorough assessment of the client's financial state of affairs, and see if there's anything I can help with. The second step is to profile everybody in advance to see if there's going to be a fit. And I insist upon everybody profiling us too. I want you to check us out, lift the hood, kick the tires. If there's something we can help you with, if there's a fit, then there's a possibility we can have a working relationship."

The above creates a word picture about the person's business that doesn't require braggadocio. In addition, he's applying some reverse psychology. By saying, "We have to profile everybody to see if there's a fit," he's suggesting that the prospect might not qualify. The implication is, "We never talk anybody into doing business with us." This takes a high degree of skill, and demonstrates why this person is extremely successful at marketing his services to the affluent. And all of this was derived from knowing how to ask and field questions.

Watch for Red Flags

Telling the prospect that you want to make sure there's a fit that you need to make certain you can meet their needs, that you can handle the job, which you need to make certain the product is really what they're looking for isn't just clever psychology. It's also for your own protection. You should always present yourself as if you were screening prospects, for their benefit, since you don't want to waste their time. And you don't want to waste *your* time either. So, keep your eyes peeled for red flags! A good salesperson watches for any number of warnings indicating that an affluent prospect will be a time waster rather than a good client. Remember, the affluent consumer works more hours than most people. The last thing they want is to waste time.

For instance, some prospects will harbor unrealistic expectations of what you can and cannot do. Recently, a friend told me that his sister wanted the outside of her 6,500 square foot house painted for $1,500, because she'd read somewhere that house painters were "notorious rip-offs." She received three bids, and none were anywhere close (the lowest bid was about $8,500). At the time of this writing, her house still needs painting, and everyone's time has been wasted. Good luck.

Be leery of the affluent prospect who demands to know what you charge before you've uncovered her true needs. Like the lady wanting her house painted for $1,500, this needs to be handled skillfully. "What's your fee, what do you charge?" Those who are most successful in marketing to the affluent rarely discuss prices with an unsold prospect—in fact, hardly ever.

If possible, seamlessly shift conversation in order to uncover needs. A landscaper might simply say, "First I'll need to spend about an hour with you on your property, and then create a plan based on what you're looking for." A financial advisor might say, "Before I can answer that question, I need to make a thorough assessment of your financial affairs to determine where and if I can help."

Whenever possible, you do *not* want to get sucked into a premature fee discussion. I've watched even seasoned professionals fall into this trap many times. Whether they're selling luxury cars, financial advice or home security systems, salespeople who get sucked into premature price discussions end up wasting time or selling based on price alone.

It is important to remember that discounting fees is statistically insignificant when it comes to affluent loyalty. And affluent client loyalty is the most significant criteria for stimulating positive word-of-mouth influence. Don't allow the old cliché, *price is only a consideration in the absence of value*, to kick into gear.

This holds true in virtually every forum. Hal, an entertainment center specialist, succeeded despite the fact that he worked for a large electronics/entertainment chain that constantly advertised specials in order to lure people into the store. His customers thought they would spend $2,500 for an advertised unit, but because Hal asked the right questions, knew how to listen, and was skilled at summarizing and explaining complicated products, his average ticket was closer to $10,000 per customer.

Other than the first encounter, where prospective customers asked to see the products being advertised at specific discounted prices, Hal never discussed price until he was certain they were sold on his complete entertainment center. The other salespeople sold to the asking price.

Proving Your Competence

You must have the skills to demonstrate your competence without coming off as a jargon-spewing know-it-all. You want to demonstrate your expertise in a casual, conversational way. If you really know your stuff (and you'd better), you must learn how to present that knowledge so that anyone with a 12th grade education can understand.

If you've successfully developed rapport, you now know something about the other person. You've done your homework before the meeting, listened and learned during the meeting, and gathered enough "intel." Now you're positioned to probe deeper, and let individuals talk about their favorite subjects—themselves, their successes and their goals. As you develop rapport, they discover reasons to like you, and the process of building trust begins. Trust has to be earned over time, so you're just initiating the process. And you initiate the process by being sincere and engaging.

Most of all, you are proving your competency by the seamless nature of your sales skills. When it's your turn to speak, you're able to create a simple and succinct word picture about what you do and how you can help them create the future they want.

Making the Sale

Although a good sales professional is never timid about asking for business, she never asks for it prematurely. She waits until she's earned that emotional equity, until she's accrued some professional respect from demonstrating her competence. Only then will she say, "Brian, I'd like the opportunity to be your trusted insurance provider" or "Brian, I'd like to talk business with you." Sometimes, she'll just say, "Let's get started."

Whenever there's an objection, she stops, goes back, and addresses the issue directly. At this point, she might realize that she needs to develop a better rapport, or that she hasn't been clear enough. But she will be persistent. She's not going to let an opportunity get away without a fight. The best salesperson is an expert at closing the deal, but she doesn't make it complicated. She keeps it simple.

Eduardo is a true rainmaker flourishing in the sphere of affluence. He is a legal Mexican immigrant and the owner of a lucrative house painting business. English will always be a second language, which could easily be perceived as a major obstacle—especially when no one in his crew is very conversant outside his native language—but Eduardo has mastered the art of marketing to the affluent. His entire business has been built on positive word-of-influence. It began six years ago when two high-end real estate agents hired him to prep a couple of luxury homes they were about to list. The objective was for both the homeowner and agent to top dollar for the house. So the homeowner *and* the listing agent had a vested interest in the quality of his work.

Not only did Eduardo and his crew do excellent work, they were very professional, worked hard, completed the job in a timely manner and cleaned up after themselves every day. Using only a cell phone and a cheap business card, Eduardo stimulated positive word-of-mouth influence by asking for referrals from the homeowners and the real-estate agents. He built his affluent clientele from there.

Eduardo never quotes a price without thoroughly assessing the type of paint required and the timeline for completing the job. In his own words, "My work is always good, my price is always fair, rarely do I ever have to lower it, and then only a little—and I never lose a job." I know a few landscaping companies that could learn a lot from Eduardo.

As I have stated repeatedly, anyone who has the desire can excel in marketing and selling their services to the affluent. But you have to understand the affluent as thoroughly as the products or services that you sell. This requires work.

Research Facts

- 7% of professionals marketing their services to the affluent excel in bringing in new affluent customers / clients. —2005 Affluent Client Acquisition study
- Word-of-mouth influence has the most statistical significance in the affluent consumer's decision making—deciding who, what, and where do conduct their business. —2004 APD research
- 93% of all communication is non-verbal.
- Two serious dislikes of America's top quintile income earners include salespeople and taxes.

11

Building Relationships with the Affluent

Because the salesperson is the product, he or she has a major impact on making or breaking the sale.

—2004 Research Study,
How the Affluent Make Purchasing Decisions

Consider the following scenario.

One of your clients knows a college graduate who enjoys golf. The client asks if the young man can play along sometime, and you agree. On the day of the outing, the kid is incredibly polite and helpful, giving you pointers, raking the sand traps, holding the flags, etc. He's a pleasure.

What would a good salesperson do next?

In a real-world case, the sales professional (Tom) was so impressed with the young man that he sent a handwritten thank-you note to his wealthy father, complimenting him on his son. Obviously, that activity needed follow up, and Tom did so. He found a reason to arrange a face-to-face business meeting with the father, which involved another trip to the golf course.

What would the average salesperson do?

First, he would have found a reason *not* to golf with the client in the first place. Second, he'd be reluctant to let an unknown kid play along, since the young man isn't an ideal affluent prospect. And even if the sales pro learned that the young man's father was a person of considerable wealth, it wouldn't occur to him to send a handwritten note to the father. He'd never even *think* of reaching out to the father through the son.

Why wouldn't these thoughts occur to the average sales professional? Two reasons: (1) he hasn't performed the right prospecting activities often enough to develop the proper mindset; and (2) the skills needed to execute these prospecting activities fall outside his comfort zone.

Tom wasn't entirely comfortable sending the follow-up note, but he ploughed ahead anyway. That's true of any successful salesperson. If you wait until you feel comfortable—until your confidence grows—you'll wait forever.

In general, a lack of confidence and comfort stem from feeling intimidated by wealthy people. But there's no better way to gain confidence than practicing your skills. And you practice your skills by doing the right activities, and you refine your high-impact prospecting through trial and error. Through trial, error and effort, the best salespeople master the skills needed to develop personal relationships with the affluent.

Finessing Introductions & Referrals

How do you get introductions and referrals from affluent clients? Simple: you ask for them—but in a subtle way. Obviously, your goal is getting face-to-face with a new prospect. And unless your client is an idiot (and I'm sure that isn't the case), she's well aware of your strategic intent. Still, it's important that you frame your request for an introduction as a "meet and greet," not a pitch session. This is one of the activities that appears simple at first glance, but requires a high degree of skill. I'll illustrate the difference in the following dialog, which occurred between Bob (an affluent business owner) and a high-end copier salesman who had just closed the sale.

Copier Salesman:	"Bob, I really appreciate your business, and hope you can see all the work we did to make certain the machines are all set up properly with your network. I know there are other vendors, so we differentiate ourselves through our service."
Bob:	"I'm glad you guys were finally able to get everything working. It's my understanding that your service and tech people will be here on Friday to install the 3-hole puncher and take out the old machines."
Copier Salesman:	"That's right."
Bob:	"It's also my understanding that we've purchased an entire 24/7, soup-to-nuts service package. So we'll have no additional costs throughout the term of our lease."
Copier Salesman:	"Right. We'll take care of everything."
Bob:	"And if I want to upgrade the machines, say, 12 months before my lease is up, there won't be an additional charge as long as we upgrade to your newer machines."
Copier Salesman:	"That's right. We're here to serve you."
Bob:	"Thanks. I've got to jump on a conference call, but it sounds good to me."

Bob stands to leave when the copier salesman says . . .

Copier Salesman:	"We have a new campaign that requires me to ask for referrals, so if you run across anyone who needs copiers, here's my card. If you could recommend them to me, I'd appreciate it."
Bob:	"Sure."

Bob takes the business card to his office.

What are the odds that Bob will be thinking about giving his copier salesman a referral? Very slim. In fact, the odds are good that he'll misplace the business card by the time he gets off his call.

The copier salesman did exactly as he was trained. He executed the standard approach in attempting to generate referrals. In some instances, a more aggressive salesman might ask you to go to your rolodex and write down the contact information of three to five potential referrals that he could call. Ugh! Not in the world of the affluent.

Requesting referrals in this way is not just ineffective, but it cheapens the professionalism of the person asking. This particular copier salesperson and his service people are extremely knowledgeable, and they must be up to speed with the latest computer technology, networking systems and software applications, as well as their own products. They should *never* have to beg for business!

Meanwhile, the consultative salesperson, which is what this copier salesman actually is (but in need of affluent sales training) has already established a strong working relationship with Bob. In the process of selling, networking and fine-tuning the machines, he picked up some useful intelligence. This included: knowing who Bob's attorney is, since they printed some documents that the attorney emailed to Bob; learning the name of his accounting firm, since they also printed the CPAs emails; and discovering two doctors who regularly play golf with Bob on Wednesday afternoons, since they confirmed their tee times via email.

Armed with this intelligence, our copier salesperson, instead of apologizing and handing Bob his business card, could have said . . .

Copier Salesman: "Bob, I'm glad you're satisfied at this point, and it's my job to make certain that you're always satisfied. To that end, I'm going to write my personal cell phone number on the back of my business card. Feel free to call any time."

Bob: "Great."

Copier Salesman: By the way, I couldn't help but notice that we printed out correspondence from an attorney and a CPA. Are they local?"

Bob:	"Yeah. I'm buying a property in the mountains, and they're finishing up my paperwork."
Copier Salesman:	"I was wondering if you could introduce me to them. I'm sure they make a lot of use of their machines."
Bob:	"I'd be happy to. I'm having lunch with my attorney on Friday. If you come by with the technician and the service person, you and I can ride together."
Copier Salesman:	"Great. I'll be in your office around 11:30 this Friday."

In this scenario, the referral request is far less intrusive. The copier salesman is helping Bob to help him. He's asking to meet the attorney from a position of strength. Notice that he didn't continue his pursuit by also suggesting a meeting with Bob's CPA or golfing buddies. There will be time for that—later. In fact, the salesman should be planning to talk about the CPA while driving to lunch, or during lunch with the attorney. The doctor golfing buddies will be kept for later contact.

Is it that simple? Yes.

Is it that easy? Not always. If it was, everyone would be doing it.

The well-trained consultative salesperson asks directly for the introduction, but packages it in a non-threatening way. He understands that less is better—less verbiage, less foreplay, less dancing around the issue of getting face-to-face. He has mastered the skills of being both subtle and direct.

The affluent, whether they're business owners, attorneys, CPAs or physicians, don't want an overly eager salesperson pigeonholing them and pitching their wares. The most successful salespeople are always subtle, but never too subtle. For example, our copier salesman might say, "Don't hesitate to sing my praises to your attorney if he asks." This proactively stimulates positive word-of-mouth influence. It's subtle but direct, with everything linked to the long-term objective of generating future affluent business.

Be Yourself . . . at Your Best

Selling to the affluent begins with refining your image. Your personality, your image and your first impression on the prospect are extremely important. The best sales professional pays careful attention to his grooming and dress. He doesn't overdress, but he *never* under-dresses. (When in doubt, play it safe by dressing up a half-notch.)

This holds true in every aspect of marketing and selling to the affluent. For example, ADT Custom Home Services was spawned to fill the increasing demands of affluent home owners. Greg Norman has been hired as their spokesperson, my firm has been hired to train their hand-picked reps on the art of selling to the affluent, and they are branding a new slogan (*The Gold Standard*) around all of this.

During one of our two-day workshops, I was about to discuss image and the affluent, when one of the participants asked, "How important is the way we dress to affluent home owners?" My response: "Very important."

In their past lives as residential salespeople, ADT reps wore casual clothes (maybe a golf shirt with an ADT logo) that made them look sales reps at Target or your local wireless provider. That's acceptable attire for normal retail sales, but a bit sloppy for gold-standard professionals selling to the affluent. Fortunately, my questioner saved me any embarrassment by suggesting that he should probably upgrade his wardrobe to sport coats, dress slacks, good shoes and button-down shirts and ties. I agreed.

Nine months after that training session, I was talking with the Director of ADT Custom Home Services, and asked about the customer rep who said he was going to upgrade his wardrobe. What I heard was music to any coach's ears: "He's knocking the cover off the ball! He upgraded his entire image, and his sales have gone through the roof."

This Custom Home Service sales force has become elite group who, rather than simply selling units, is completely consultative. Each rep now "designs security systems for a select group of families in their territory." And, I'm proud to say, the results of my training on how to market to the affluent have been outstanding.

Of course, "image" goes beyond dress, and the true professional understands fundamental social graces. ADT's elite customer reps frequently find themselves breaking bread with clients (formerly referred to as customers), and have been forced to pay closer attention to some of the finer points of social etiquette.

This is not simply an ADT gold standard issue: in another industry, one of my female clients attended a finishing school to boost her confidence. For her, it wasn't a matter of merely distinguishing between various spoons and forks at formal dinner parties, but learning the ABCs of formal dress and etiquette—just in case. She even went as far as practicing in front of a mirror and visualizing each encounter. More than anything else, this served to build her confidence so she could apply the skills she was learning.

Recently a daughter of a good friend, armed with her new MBA, went on a final job interview—"a formality that involved having dinner with the big boss at a fancy restaurant," said my friend. Apparently, his daughter was nervous about the etiquette of this event, convinced it was her final test prior to being offered a job. Since I knew her fairly well, my advice was both personal and simple. I told her to be herself, make certain she relaxed as much as possible, and to watch her boss whenever she was in doubt about which utensil to use. I didn't think she was much of a drinker, but I suggested she avoid alcohol, order easy-to-eat food (i.e., not messy) and forego a "doggie-bag" if there were any leftovers.

I later learned that she passed the dinner interview with flying colors and was offered an employment contract shortly afterwards. However, my advice regarding alcohol and doggie-bags has become a family joke. Apparently, the daughter was dining with four of the big bosses' direct reports, one being her future supervisor. The dinner began at the bar because the big boss was a serious drinker, consuming three martinis before they were seated at their table. When the menus arrived, bottles of wine were ordered immediately. At the end of the meal, there were volumes of leftovers, and everyone asked for doggie-bags. So, with one glass of wine in her belly and a doggie-bag in hand, my friend's daughter passed her etiquette test with flying colors. Go figure.

The moral of the story is: learn how to be comfortable in your own skin, and understand the rules of engagement for a variety of situations. Social self-consciousness can cause much unnecessary embarrassment. It's amazing how many people are intimidated by status. They walk into a fancy restaurant, and they're too self-conscious to be themselves. You don't have to be perfectly aligned to all of the little idiosyncrasies of the country club or whatever, but you have to be confident that you won't make a fool of yourself. It's simple, but it requires you to be yourself—not someone you think you should be.

Trying Too Hard

When salespeople feel out-of-place, many end up violating the basic rules of human engagement because they try too hard. You'll also encounter this in other social situations where self-consciousness is present. In such circumstances, people tend to display one of two behaviors: (1) they try to dominate the conversation, or (2) they don't even enter the conversation. When it comes to interacting with affluent boomers, attempting to dominate the conversation (which in any circle is a sign that someone is trying to show off) is absolutely the wrong behavior. Remember, it is your responsibility to make your affluent prospects, clients and customers feel comfortable around you.

You do not want to get too personal, and you must be careful with your humor. Even if you're one of those people who find humor in almost anything and have a knack for making people laugh, be careful. When the affluent are in decision-making mode, they want you to assist them in this process. They are not looking for a new friend or someone to make them laugh.

Work on your communication skills and your ability to build relationships with idiosyncratic affluent strangers. I know: easier said than done, but it's very do-able, which is critical when we venture into the affluent world of strategic networking.

Strategic Networking

The more we become addicted to the advances in technology, the greater our need for personal interaction. The busier the affluent become, the more they get involved with outside activities that allow them to socialize, possibly be of assistance to others, and hopefully get something out of it for themselves. The bottom line is that everyone networks to some degree. The affluent merely tend to do *more* networking (and at higher levels).

That's because the affluent have more money and, in general, are naturally drawn to groups of people with a similar lifestyle. We enjoy being with people who share our interests and concerns—people who play where we play. Although there has been much discussion regarding various networking categories (and Facebook and MySpace have brought the next generation into the game via the Internet), for our purposes, networking groups still fall into three basic categories:

- *Social Groups*—Here is where the affluent get together to have fun, blow-off steam, and release some of the stress they have been carrying around. Because they are social in nature, the affluent are drawn together because of the activities, enjoyment and—quite frequently—the prestige a particular group provides.
- *Community Groups*—Partly because the link between aging and retirement is eroding (mandatory retirement was eliminated in 1986) and partly because the affluent have not saved enough, affluent boomers—the children of the so-called "Greatest Generation"—have done less by every measure of civic involvement, including rates of voting and joining community groups.

  With that reality in mind, community groups remain one of the three basic categories for networking. Today, you will be drawn together with the more civic-minded affluent boomers who, like you, are focused on contributing to the local community.
- *Industry Groups*—Members of these groups are more inclined to discuss business, but keep in mind that the affluent who participate are also interested in learning and pursuing *personal* inter-

ests related to the technology and culture within their chosen field.

As you consider the possibilities associated with strategic networking, remember that the affluent make major purchase decisions through word-of-mouth influence—by asking the opinions of people they respect and trust, on very specific matters. Obviously, this word-of-mouth influence works both ways: it can be positive or negative.

What has become a natural part of their decision making process has inadvertently "upped" their motivation to participate in such groups—"Maybe Dr. Fields will be there, I need to talk to him about Amber's knee." It gives these social groups a different intent.

Your first step is to identify the social, community and industry groups in which affluent boomers (either current or prospective customers or clients) participate. This is not a difficult process:

- First, do your homework and outline the social, community and industry groups active in your community.
- Second, segment those groups into the handful you would think your affluent customers/clients might participate in, if they were involved.
- Third, ask your customers/clients about the specific groups that you've identified. You want to uncover which groups are most populated by your clientele.
- Fourth, select one group and ask one of your customers/clients if he would take you as a guest.

Your mission is to become a known, respected and trusted member of whatever group(s) you decide to get involved with. Your involvement will become your calling card within the group. If orchestrated properly, word-of-mouth influence should eventually circulate throughout the group, and individuals will seek out your services, which will quickly evolve into additional introductions and referrals to the people they know.

Let me give you a quick "Cliffs Notes" overview of how this works.

Social Groups

Golfing events, fishing trips, sporting events, weddings. . . . The list of social events goes on and on, but the concept is simple. Your first step is to gain entry into a certain group(s) through a customer/client or a good personal friend. Whoever arranges your first invitation will most likely become an *internal advocate.* This individual will introduce you to everyone, explain the ins and outs of the group, and will help identify people who match your *Affluent Prospect Profile.*

Most important, whenever getting involved socially, take the time to develop a natural rapport with the people you meet. You only have one shot at making a good first impression, and many salespeople blow it when socializing with the affluent. They blow it by being too forward—by handing out business cards too quickly, and making it generally obvious that they're present only to solicit business from members. This is a major faux pas. Remember that these mature affluent boomers have an extreme dislike of being sold, and they hate being manipulated. Whenever a member senses anything but the purest of intentions, word gets around the group, and the person guilty of this infraction is exposed. Not a good situation for any professional marketing his or her products or services to the affluent.

The idea is to meet people, develop rapport (make certain they like you) and enjoy yourself. Leave your business cards in your pocket until people hand you their cards, and even then, you're better off writing your contact information on the back of their business cards. The idea is to have fun while keeping your professional hat fully in place. Do your homework about the group, learn as much as possible about the members, and be very clear on how you introduce yourself. People are always asking, "What kind of work do you do?" Be prepared to respond with a brief statement, often referred to as an elevator speech, such as . . .

"I design security systems for some of the larger homes in the area."

"I design and install entertainment systems for families in the area.

"I plan and organize large weddings."

"I handle finances for some of the families in town."

When introduced to the "right" people, your goal should be to *connect* with them at a social level and not get pigeonholed as someone hawking wedding services, entertainment systems, or whatever. Engage everyone you meet in friendly conversation. Ask more than you tell. Find out everything you can in the brief time you have with them—and most of all, make certain your internal advocate gets you invited back.

Community Groups

Because our affluent boomers pale in comparison to their parent's generation regarding civic involvement, community groups provide a real opportunity to expand your affluent centers-of-influence. Not only will you meet people who are giving back to the community, you will be able to connect with them on a personal level. This often develops into social interaction.

It is important to remember that community groups are designed to serve a purpose. The participants get involved because they support what the group represents. You must not only support what the group represents, but be willing to get involved. These affluent boomers know they are in the minority, are proud of it, and join these community organizations for one overall objective: to give back to the community.

As a result, they are drawn to other members who demonstrate a similar commitment through their participation in committees, fundraisers and other activities that advance the organization's purposes. This gives you an opportunity to position yourself within this affluent group in a very meaningful way.

You may find a few members that you can approach on a business level when you first meet, but more often, you'll first need to earn their trust. Your dedication to, and involvement in, the organization is the best way to do that.

Follow the same protocol I outlined with Social Groups. Do your homework, get invited by a member who will introduce you to everyone, get this member to become your internal advocate, get involved, and use a similar process for developing rapport, discussing business, using business cards and using your elevator speech.

Abide by the "law of reciprocity" as you consider your involvement in a civic organization. The more you give, the more you get. Your focus should be on working alongside other members to build rapport, demonstrate your dependability and establish friendships. That's the wellspring from which your business opportunities will emerge.

The following is a partial listing of some of the more familiar community organizations:

- Alumni associations
- Chambers of commerce
- Charities
- Civic organizations
- Cultural organizations
- Economic clubs
- Fraternal organizations
- Hospitals and other medical charities
- Museums
- Professional organizations
- Social service charities

Select an organization with care. The following five questions will serve as a litmus test:

1. Do the purpose and goals of this organization capture your interest? If not, it will be difficult to stay involved. Think about (or check into) the purpose behind each type of organization listed above. Which ones attract your interest?
2. Do the group's activities and events attract affluent individuals? Some organizations include wealthy people on their rolls, but not at their functions.
3. Does the organization provide opportunities to meet new people on (at least) a monthly basis? Some organizations schedule events two to four times a year, which is not often enough.
4. Is this organization recognized as a positive contributor to the community? Avoid organizations that embroil themselves in controversial issues.
5. Can you afford to be involved? Go beyond basic membership fees, and check the typical cost of monthly meetings, special events and expected contributions to any fundraising activities.

Select carefully, participate wisely and the rewards will come. You can establish significant relationships through many small involvements. And you can offer to provide professional expertise when an individual opens that window of opportunity—always suggesting a separate face-to-face meeting where "talking business" will be appropriate.

Industry Groups

This strategy is often referred to as *industry immersion*, and that's a good description of what will occur. There are several reasons why it's ideal for you to pursue industry groups.

- As a professional, it makes perfect sense to take special interest in an industry that you believe is vital to your area's economic development.
- Becoming connected to a corporate community will put you in direct contact with affluent prospects, resulting in new clients and referrals to their associates.
- Because this is a business environment, it often takes less time to "get down to business" with the people you contact—versus social and community groups. People are ready to talk business, and expect business relationships to emerge from those conversations.

Begin by contacting your local Chamber of Commerce and other organizations that are leading economic development efforts in your area. Meet with individuals in those organizations who are personally connected to those efforts. There are a number of angles from which to approach these business groups. The following is merely a partial list:

- The *anchor industry(ies)* in your area—the one(s) considered to be at the heart of your community's economic future. When members mention an industry, ask why they believe that industry is a catalyst for economic development. Listen for factors such as shifting economic indicators, consumer preferences, innovation, regulatory changes, geopolitical realignment and anything else suggesting that a specific industry is a good choice.
- The *leading and emerging company(ies)* in that industry—the one(s) they believe will be at the forefront of the economic

development effort. Again, ask why they selected each company. Listen for connections to the same factors mentioned when discussing the anchor industry(ies). You may discover that the largest company is not the industry leader, and especially not the emerging leader.

- *Arrange a Tour of Company Facilities.* This is an excellent way to meet key executives and learn vital inside information, but it's important that those introductions be arranged prior to your tour. An internal advocate could be suggested by clients, family members, friends, colleagues or acquaintances. From your involvement in social and community groups, you may know (or know of) a key individual who works for, or serves on the board, of the company you've targeted, or who personally knows a senior executive. This is an important element of a successful company tour, so keep searching until you find the right person.
- *Attend Industry Conferences.* These events tend to attract the hard-working affluent who are looking for new ideas, new technologies, and to meet new people. Enter the words "conference" and the specific industry name in your favorite Internet search engine to learn more about conferences they suggest—or to identify other conferences that might be of interest to you. Conference websites frequently list speakers and the companies that have booked display booth space. Research these speakers and companies to uncover information that will help you introduce yourself to the people you really want to know. Also, whenever possible you will want to stay either in the hotel where the conference is being held, or within walking distance. You want to make it easy to network!
- *Attend Annual Shareholder Meetings.* These are showcases. The intent is to present the company in a favorable light to shareholders. Management is typically eager to impress attendees, since most will be affluent to some degree. Also, people who may be otherwise difficult to reach will often be there.

These efforts to immerse yourself in a vital industry will lead you to other introductions and referrals as well—to customers and suppliers of the companies where you're making inroads, and to the social and community groups to which key people in those companies are connected.

Strategic Referral Alliances

Not all referrals need come from satisfied customers or clients. Many strong referral alliances are established among professionals whose services are connected. There are countless examples of how these alliances work and how they are inter-connected. For instance . . .

A high-end historic home renovation company has numerous preferred referral alliances: home entertainment and smart wiring as part of the renovation project, and an interior decorator who helps select colors, fabrics and specific pieces of furniture.

The home entertainment professional has a strategic referral alliance with a luxury-home security consultant because he frequently, after his affluent customers recognize the value of their new "smart" home and entertainment center, gets inquiries about protecting the home against fire and theft.

The high-end historic home renovation company also has a strategic referral alliance with a company the lays cement for patios and driveways.

Most family dentists have an alliance with both an oral surgeon and an orthodontist. Our family physician referred my daughter Amy to an orthopedic surgeon after she tore her ACL in a skiing accident. My wife's personal trainer refers her students to a nutritionist.

CPAs typically have a few attorneys and financial advisors and planners they recommend. The idea is to establish these types of alliances with professionals who provide complementary, but non-competitive, products and services to the affluent people within the target market.

When you meet with any professional to explore a strategic referral alliance, you must establish a mutual understanding on three key points.

- How you can bring value to their customer/client relationships by being knowledgeable, trustworthy and dependable. You will make them look good.
- How you work very hard to establish long-term relationships within affluent circles, and will reciprocate with affluent referrals whenever possible.
- How you seek the same type of long-term relationship with your strategic referral alliance partners.

Approach each potential referral alliance as you would any professional relationship. Honor all commitments, and serve the other person well, adding value whenever possible. After you have begun a Strategic Referral Alliance, the following strategy will help you maximize the value of the relationship:

- Commit to serving your customer/clients, alliance partners and referred prospects extremely well. Provide true value that exceeds expectations. Nurture relationships of trust.
- Make certain that you are clear about your *Ideal Affluent Client-Prospect Profile.*
- Give generously, both to your customers/clients and your strategic alliance partner, believing that the benefits will come.
- After you contact a referral, keep your strategic referral alliance partner fully informed of your progress with that prospect.
- Always carry the attitude of winning new friends and positively influencing people you come in contact with.

Intimate Client Events

Intimate client events serve two purposes. The key is to never lose sight of the primary purpose—to show your appreciation to your best clients. The secondary purpose is to get introductions to the friends, family and colleagues of these top clients.

A tremendous benefit of strengthening the loyalty of your best clients is the solicited and unsolicited introductions they provide to people with similar financial situations. Since affluent investors make most of their decisions through word-of-mouth influence, strategically crafted intimate client events become a wonderful platform for stimulating that influence. Be strategic about the clients you invite and the people you want them to invite. Shoot for around 12–16 people at the event. Ideally, this total would comprise half clients and half guests.

Many types of events can be used: a dinner, golf outing, personal growth seminar, outdoor barbecue—the list goes on. If you aren't certain about ideas for an event, ask your clients for their opinions. Be guided by your clients' interests and your own imagination. We will use a wine tasting as our example. The following contact points provide rich opportunities to express your appreciation before, during and after the event, while executing high-impact rainmaking activities (face-to-face):

- The initial phone call to invite clients (and their spouses), explain the nature of the event (wine tasting, pure fun—no business), insist they bring (name of affluent prospect in the Center of Influence, if available) or a good friend, or someone we'd like to meet. Emphasize that there will be NO business, and that this is simply how you meet people and express your appreciation to good clients.
- The confirmation letter you send to those who accept (optional).
- The reminder phone call 2–3 days before the event.
- The actual wine-tasting portion of the event.
- Use a digital camera to photograph the event in progress.
- Collect e-mail contacts before the wine tasting so you can send photos and wine information after the event.
- The time of mingling before, during and after the event.
- The guests all depart with a small gift—e.g., a wine book, wine case, bottle of wine, etc.
- The follow-up call to your clients 2–3 days following the event.

An intimate client event builds loyalty by making the client feel appreciated at each one of those points of contact. Here are some tips on how to make that happen:

1. Plan two or three events at future dates over a 3–5 month period. Set the dates, book the facilities, and arrange the programs for all three—before you begin making calls for the first event. When you call to invite clients to the first event, you will have two later events they can attend if the first date is no good for them. You should begin those phone calls about 3–4 weeks ahead of the first event. **Do not initially invite clients by letter!**
2. Limit the number of clients you invite to a given event. Make certain you can have a personal conversation with each client and prospect sometime during the event.
3. The confirmation letter should include complete information on location and parking, plus an expression of your enthusiasm about their being able to join you for this event.
4. Before the event, plan with your team to make certain no one is ever left alone during the event. The critical times are the informal mingling before the event and as everyone leaves. Plan to make certain everyone is receiving adequate attention at all times.
5. The quality of the location, wine tasting and activities won't be noticed by your clients—*unless* any one of them is mediocre or poor. The location must be just right; the wine should be of good quality and not undesirable to anyone, and the event (1 to 2 hours maximum) should be universally enjoyable. Everything must say, "Because we appreciate you, we care enough to give you the very best."
6. Promptly send the photographs taken at the event. Attach a personal message to each e-mail referencing the event and any "surprise-and-delight" information you uncovered about them. "Jim, thanks for coming, I know it's not like watching your Yankees play, but it looks like you (and your wife Nancy, friend Joe, etc.) were having a great time in the third picture."
7. Unless you have a very good reason to do otherwise, the follow-up call to clients 2–3 days after the event should be devoid of business. Instead, it should consist of a simple "thanks for coming, we were honored by your presence" exchange. This is an ex-

cellent opportunity to reference the pictures you took with your digital camera.

If you already have something of a business nature in the works, and want to include it in your call, say something like:

"First of all, I wanted to tell you how much we enjoyed having you at the wine tasting on Monday night. We were truly honored by your presence."

"Also, we have a quarterly review meeting scheduled for Friday at 3:00 p.m., and I want to make certain that was still OK with you."

A well-planned event leads to predictable behaviors—including the additional business and referrals loyal clients provide for you.

When using high-impact prospecting methods, your objective is to get to know qualified prospects, get them to like you and respect your professional competence, and begin to establish trust. All of this is necessary before they'll be ready to "talk business." Once they reach that point, however, not only will they be ready for a long-term relationship, they may be ready to serve as an internal advocate.

Ask questions—lots of questions. Look for things you have in common. Search for ways to become involved in activities and events that interest them. Find ways to help and support them. Most of all: be patient.

As the relationship evolves, they will discover what you do and begin thinking about how this relates to their needs, and the needs of people important to them. At the same time, you will also uncover those needs, and determine when the time is right to approach them on a professional level.

The most successful sales professionals understand this.

That's why these methods have such high impact.

Research Facts

High Impact Activities

- Arranging Introductions
- Getting Referrals
- Strategic Networking
- Strategic Referral Alliances
- Intimate Client Events

12

12 Commandments of Understanding the Affluent

1. **Know thyself**—You must be comfortable in your own skin to truly become a master of the top quintile. Whether you are aspiring to become affluent or you're already affluent according to the U.S. Census Bureau, it's important to recognize your personal strengths, weaknesses, goals, dreams and immediate aspirations as they relate to understanding the affluent. If you are reading this handbook, odds are that you're either already in the top quintile of U.S. income earners or soon to enter the top quintile.

   The odds are also good that you're the product of a middle-class upbringing and have wholesome middle-class values and aspirations deeply imprinted into your subconscious. And there is a distinct probability that as much as this handbook will help you market and sell your goods and services to affluent consumers, it will also help you understand yourself. Your motivators are likely to be very similar, if not identical, to those of your affluent clients and prospects. The stress you feel in your efforts to provide a comfortable lifestyle for your family is exactly the stress that the affluent feel. The services you crave, they crave. Feel their pain, empathize with them, and be yourself.

2. **Be a Lifelong Learner**—Understanding the affluent is not for the lazy, faint of heart or people who jump to conclusions before gathering the requisite knowledge. When it comes to marketing to the

affluent, or living life to its fullest, you can learn and grow every day, or slowly die as your brain atrophies. Because the affluent have so much money, nearly every aspect of Western capitalism involves them—directly or indirectly.

Not only do you need to be a student of the affluent, you need to be a student—period! I'll bet you have little time or tolerance for the shallow and uninformed. And I'd wager that you work hard to avoid boring people. Ditto your affluent clients and prospects. The broader your base of knowledge, the more varied your interests, the greater your understanding of life. This will also enhance your confidence and make navigating the "sphere of affluence" more pleasurable.

In the words of Charlie Munger, Warren Buffet's partner, "I've never met a wise person who didn't read books." Enough said.

3. **Be Willing to Serve**—I don't know you, but I *do* know that you like to be served, whether in an upscale restaurant, a deli, Nordstroms or Target; whether you're dealing with your dentist, CPA or financial advisor; whether you're visiting the Department of Motor Vehicles, the U.S. Post Office or your local police department. You want good service. Actually, you DEMAND good service! And when you fail to get good service, something that's become all-too commonplace, you get annoyed.

The affluent crave superior service. They are addicted to it, but most are in denial. Even though many affluent boomers have a gritty, meat-and-potatoes, workingman ideal stamped into their subconscious, they *really* want to be coddled, fussed over and served at all levels. They work hard to service their customers, and they demand the same treatment when it's their turn to be the consumer.

You will experience the power of this commandment in your family, in your friendships, working with colleagues, as well as in marketing and selling your wares. The more you are willing to serve, the more you will gain in your dealings with the affluent. The law of reciprocity is alive and well in our top quintile.

4. **Be Personal**—Although the affluent may not be actively looking for new friends, one of the key commandments for maintaining a healthy and enduring relationship is that the affluent must get to know you. As simple as this might appear, our research indicates that this is a serious challenge when dealing with the affluent. Too many people put on airs, try too hard to project an image that they think the affluent will like, and go through life in fear of their "fraud" being discovered. Successfully selling to the affluent is just a matter of being yourself, but also of presenting the best "self" you have to offer.

   The affluent want to feel they have a personal connection with you. The more you are able to be comfortable in your own skin, the more likely you are to make a personal connection with mature affluent boomers. Just think how impersonal your life as an affluent consumer has become. You purchase a warranty and then have to call an 800 number and talk to someone on the other side of the world to handle your issue. These customer services reps all sound the same, read from the same script, and as you're about to hang-up because of this frustrating experience, you're asked, "Is there anything else I can help you with?" The 21st Century has become so impersonal that the affluent have developed a strong psychological need for personal interaction.

5. **Be Likeable**—It's hard to imagine taking time to get personal with prospects and clients while overlooking the need to make yourself likeable, but it happens. Sadly, many affluent boomers are so self-absorbed that they don't recognize how they are perceived by others.

   You may be thinking, "This commandment should go without saying." And if this thought just flitted through your mind, I agree! However, all we have to do is keep our ears open in congested areas and it won't be long before you hear affluent arrogance at its best. Just the other day, I experienced a travel day from Hell—flights canceled, weather delays, etc. I was at the counter desperately trying to fly "stand-by" on the next flight, when the airline attendant and I were rudely interrupted by the sound of "Excuse me! I'm a Chairman's Preferred customer (U.S. Airlines' highest status), and I'm guaranteed a seat on any flight. Sir—you need to get me on this flight—I'm a Chairman's Preferred, and I'm guaranteed a seat!"

He made a fool of himself in front of everyone, and because I simply looked on in amusement, once this rude traveler departed, the attendant thanked me for being so understanding, and although both the rude flyer and I got on the same flight, I was seated first. I must confess: I enjoyed my small victory.

Here's the irony: like many affluent boomers, our rude flyer annoyed everyone with his self-absorbed arrogance, but didn't *perceive* himself as such. He smiled and shrugged as he walked past me to his seat on the plane. I didn't get the chance to talk with him, but I'd wager that deep inside, he's just like you and me.

This is often the case. No matter how arrogant affluent boomers might appear, they actually want to be liked. And you want them to like you. Because of the schizophrenic nature of our top quintile, you can only build a strong and lasting relationship with them if—after they get to know you on a personal level—they have determined that they like you. It pays to be nice.

6. **Be Trustworthy**—Because the affluent are so skeptical and distrusting, it's essential to do everything in your power to convey trustworthiness. You will only get so far if the affluent get to know you and like you, but (for whatever reason) don't quite trust you. Nobody places much value in superficial relationships, and the affluent have numerous relationships of this nature. Little things mean everything when it comes to trust. Say what you're going to do and DO what you say. Never make promises or commitments that you aren't 100% certain you can keep. And always tell the truth. If our savvy affluent boomers catch you in one misstatement (lie), they know you will lie to them again. Hence, they will never fully trust you. Be honest, courteous and kind. Earn their trust, and you will take these relationships to another dimension.

7. **Earn Respect**—If you want to gain influence in the sphere of affluence, it's imperative to acquire their respect. And respect has to be earned through your actions. This goes beyond trust and likeability. This requires a broad knowledge base and a willingness to help. From a business standpoint, it requires top-quality products and services. Also, it involves putting your self-interest second to their interests.

8. **Be Flexible**—Because the affluent often comprise a variety of contradictions, it's important to quickly shift gears as you're presented with each contradiction. The stress of dual-income earners working hard to maintain their affluent lifestyles, and raise children and grandchildren, requires that you be VERY flexible. Whether this flexibility involves responding to frequently rescheduled appointments, procrastination about major decisions or complete reversals on what they want to purchase, the secret to success is to *not* take anything personally. Instead, go with the flow.

9. **Know the Key Motivators**—Become a student of the 4 Key Motivators: personal health, family health, financial health and spiritual health. With more than 39 million boomers over age 50 at this writing, these four motivators will only become more relevant to those trying to market and sell to the top quintile.

10. **Be Time Sensitive**—Herein lies another affluent boomer contradiction. Your prospects and clients do *not* want you to waste their time, since these hard chargers recognize time as a precious commodity. Simultaneously, they want you to *spend* time with them so that they can get to know you better. Bottom line: the more time you spend with the affluent, without wasting their time or being a complete bore, the easier it will be develop strong relationships. In turn, this will provide you with a healthy dose of experiential knowledge.

11. **Develop Thick Skin**—You need to be immunized to the slights and faux pas of demanding, mature affluent boomers. They don't really mean to be rude, curt or discourteous (most of the time), but it

just happens. Oftentimes, some external factor has elevated their already high stress levels, which causes them to snap. You need to have thick skin when dealing with the affluent—whether on a business or personal level. The affluent are often so self-absorbed that they can be unwittingly rude and discourteous.

12. **Enjoy the Affluent**—Have fun with them. Once they get to know you, like you and trust you—the affluent world is your oyster.

Index

About The Oechsli Institute

The Oechsli Institute, founded in 1978, is one of the leading authorities regarding marketing, selling, servicing and earning loyalty with affluent clients. They have conducted numerous research projects on the affluent. From this research, The Oechsli Institute has developed a number of training options:

Keynotes and Workshops
The Oechsli Institute does countless speaking engagements every year – all customized and tailored to your organization and time frame. All the information presented is research based, action oriented, and street tested.

Rainmaker Weekends
Rainmaker Weekends are 2-day action packed workshops for sales professionals who are serious about acquiring affluent clients. Learn how to better attract, service, and retain affluent clients—all based on 7 years of comprehensive research. These Weekends involve role-playing, specific do's and don'ts, all of which are important for affluent sales success.

Customized Research Projects
The Oechsli Institute conducts ongoing research projects. They also conduct customized research projects for companies and organizations.

High Performance Teams
The Oechsli Institute has conducted a comprehensive four year research project that explored the performance factors of approximately 1,000 teams. They have since developed numerous programs designed to help teams progress through the predictable stages of team development to higher levels of performance.

Performance Coaching
The Oechsli Institute works with individuals and teams who want to improve their ability to attract, service, and develop loyal affluent clients. Their clients work in collaborative relationships with a certified coach, are committed to action, and eager to experience serious growth.

Books, CDs, and DVDs
The Oechsli Institute has dozens of books, CDs, DVDs, and packages designed to improve your ability to sell to the affluent. *The Art of Selling to the Affluent* is an industry best-seller.

For more information, contact The Oechsli Institute:

The Oechsli Institute
www.Oechsli.com
info@oechsli.com
(800) 883-6582